Core Elements

Stephen Olar

CORE ELEMENTS

Bibleschooldropout@gmail.com

Print Copy ISBN: 978-0-9877292-4-8

Electric Copy ISBN: 978-0-9920608-5-5

Other titles Available at Amazon.com

Bible Studies:

Other titles Available at Amazon.com

Bible Studies:

The Bible School Dropout's Bigger and Better Guide to Bible Study - Print and E-book editions available.

The Bible School Dropout's Guide to More Bible Study – Print and E-book editions available

The Bible School Dropout's Guide to Building the Word of God in My Life - Print and E-book editions available

The Bible School Dropout's Guide to Hebrews

The Bible School Dropout's Guide to Dispensationalism

The Bible School Dropout's Book of Charts

The Bible School Dropout's Guide to Genesis 1-11

The Bible School Dropout's Guide to Genesis 12-26

In Hot Pursuit: Twelve Things God Wants Us to Pursue – Print and E-Book versions.

Xtreme Xianity – Print and E-Book versions available

Core Elements – Print and E-book versions available

The Name of the Lord is... Volume One: Pretty Awesome, Great, Glorious and Like Totally Excellent! - Print and E-books versions available

The Name of the Lord is... Volume Two: Hi! I'm God - Print and E-book versions available

The Name of the Lord is... Volume 2.5: Hi! I'm still God. – Print and E-book versions available

The Name of the Lord is... Volume Three: The Great I Am - Print and E-books versions available

Novels:

Free – Print and E-book editions available

Icthus – Print and E-book editions available

Table of Contents

Introduction

The quest for the perfect body takes perseverance. You have to eat properly and spend a lot of time at the gym, doing workouts designed to sculpt and tone your body into perfect shape. An important part of any exercise regimen is designed to strengthen the muscles of our abdomen and upper body, or the core. It is not only the wash board abs we strive to achieve, but a strong core holds our skeletal structure in place. We stand straighter, look like a million bucks and feel better. When the core is strong, our organs are held in place better and function at top efficiency. When we don't exercise the core, we slouch, show off our pot belly and moan and groan at our various aches and pains.

The same principles can be applied to our spiritual lives as well. There are basic fundamentals of our Christian lives which need to be worked on regularly in order to develop a strong spiritual life. From the exercise of faith, building God's Word in our lives to witnessing and prayer; there is a common thread running through all of them which is necessary to develop a strong core for spiritual growth in our journey.

All of the topics we will be looking at in this study can be considered first steps or fundamentals of the faith. They are things we should have learned early in our Christian walk, but didn't or don't have a good understanding of them.

If you have done a Bible School Dropout study before, the format hasn't changed. Each topic we study is comprised a series of small studies. *Core Elements* has a two-fold purpose. While we are studying the main topics, I am also presenting each lesson in such a way to teach you Bible study methods as well. I usually leave most of my opinion out of my studies. I want you to study the Scriptures for yourself and come to your own conclusions on the topics under discussion.

I am not an expert on the topics under discussion. They are put together based upon my experience. You may agree with the topics, or think there should be more or less or a different list all together.

This book is also not an exhaustive treatment of the topics we will be examining. There have been many books written about each of them. I have attempted to produce something which will touch on the basic concepts and open the door for you to explore them further as you continue your spiritual journey.

CORE ELEMENTS

Each of us comes to this study with our own experiences and frames of reference. If you have other information to bring into the study, feel free to work it into the lesson. The more evidence you have compiled the better conclusions and applications you will produce and the more successful you will be in implementing the goals you set for yourself.

I encourage people to take their time as they work through each lesson. Don't think you have a time limit to complete it, especially if you are doing this in a group setting. Some of the lessons will take longer to complete than other. You will be doing a variety of exercises, like word and verse studies, topical studies, questions and answers, and journal entries to name a few.

Some of the topics under discussion in *Core Elements* I have touched on in other books. So if a lesson or two or three look familiar, it means you have bought other studies of mine and have actually read them!

Thank you.

If this is your first book with me, thank you as well. I is my prayer you will have a wonderful journey as we explore core elements important to building and maintaining a strong spiritual life.

My last word of advice as we embark on this joint spiritual adventure is to have fun. That's right; have fun. Although studying God's Word is extremely important and should be taken seriously, we should also enjoy the experience. If doing a Bible study is boring, then you are doing the wrong study.

I hope you enjoy Core Elements as much as I have in writing it.

Stephen Olar

Wednesday, January 01, 2014

A Crash Course in Inductive Bible Study

There are many different ways to approach The Bible. From closing your eyes, opening the Book and sticking your finger on a random verse to doing a word-by-word analysis (exegesis), and all points in between. People have used many ways to study the Bible. Some of these ways are more successful than others. This study is based upon inductive study methods.

This chapter is for those of you who have decided to do this study without the benefit of knowing what Inductive Bible study is or how to do it. If you are interested in learning how to do it, may I recommend my how to guides for your enjoyment and enlightenment: *The Bible School Dropout's Bigger and Better Guide to Bible Study* and *The Bible School Dropout's Guide to More Bible Study*.

I encourage you to buy those books not only because I wrote them, although that is a very good reason, but they show the step by step process in how inductive Bible study works and you will have a better understanding of what is going on in this book and how to do it.

A Quick Definition of Inductive Reasoning and How it Works for Bible Study

Inductive Bible study is based upon the principles of inductive reasoning. Who'd a thought it! Inductive reasoning is based upon making conclusions after examining as much data as possible. The conclusion(s) reached are verifiable in terms of future experience only if all possible data has been examined. Take for example the following premise: All crows that we have observed are black. The conclusion reached is: Therefore all crows are black.

We can't be certain that a white crow will not be found in the future, but based on past observations we can conclude that this would be unlikely.

Surveys or opinion polls are great examples of inductive reasoning. Out of x number of people interviewed a certain percentage gave answer y to the question. Therefore the same percentage would apply to the general population.

We can even see examples of inductive reasoning in the Bible. Take a look at this passage.

And He was handed the book of the prophet Isaiah. And when He had opened the book, He found the place where it was written: "The Spirit of the Lord is upon Me, Because He has anointed Me To preach the gospel to the poor; He has sent Me to heal the brokenhearted, To proclaim liberty to the captives And recovery of sight to the blind, To set at liberty those who are oppressed; To proclaim the acceptable year of the Lord." Then He closed the book, and gave it back to the attendant and sat down. And the eyes of all who were in the synagogue were fixed on Him. And He began to say to them, "Today this Scripture is fulfilled in your hearing." Luke 14:17-21

Jesus' argument was fairly straightforward. I did this stuff and I'm the one this passage is talking about. His actions were verifiable by the people who witnessed them and the chances of this changing in the future were highly unlikely.

What makes this approach ideal for Bible study is it tends to be more objective than deduction. We search the Bible and reach a conclusion based upon what we have observed rather than beginning with an assumption and looking for the support of the premises.

Is the inductive approach foolproof? Of course not, although in my experience, it comes in pretty close. You can reach an incorrect conclusion if you haven't done your research and collected as much data as you can in order to support your conclusions. In other words, the more information you gather on your subject the better the outcome.

We are "BSI's"

Many of us are familiar with or fans of the CSI television franchise. Most of us are aware the letters CSI stand for Crime Scene Investigation. The job of these people is to gather evidence in order to find out what happened, who is the victim, how did they die and who did the deed. Now take that same concept and apply it to Bible study.

When we approach Bible study inductively, we are doing much the same thing. As a Bible Scene Investigator, our job is to gather the data and arrive at a set of conclusions based on the data. Except our tools are the Bible, concordances, Bible atlases, possible commentaries, and other assorted material that is available to help you as you work through the information.

Most of the time we will be seeking the answers to the following questions: who, what, where, when, why and how.

This approach to Bible study assumes that we are going to look at the Bible in what theologian-type people call *grammatical-historical*, *normal* or *literal interpretation*. That means when we look at a passage of Scripture, we take it at face value; or look at it in normal everyday meanings unless the context of the passage indicates otherwise. We are not automatically looking for deeper spiritual meaning hidden in the words, the arrangement of the words or in anything else.

The next thing that is important to pay attention to in Bible study is **CONTEXT**. Notice I capitalized it for you and put it into bold face type. When you are studying a passage, you need to pay attention to the verses around it, the passage it is in relation to the book or letter it is in. This means taking into consideration the themes of the book, the argument the author is making and all that fun stuff. Think of context as the framework for the puzzle you are piecing together.

The first step in inductive Bible study, well, any Bible study, is *Observation*. What is the text saying? The goal is to find out information on the author, the intended audience, his theme and argument. Ask yourself questions like: What is he attempting to say to his audience? Or: Why did he use the word or phrase he did? Who was he directing this argument to? We are primarily concerned in answering the questions; what, who and sometimes where and when in the observation stage.

When the bulk of the observations are done, then it comes time to start the *Interpretation* phase. The Bible was written over 2,000 years ago to an audience having very little in common with the one reading it today--you. There are languages, cultural and historical things to be taken into consideration. There may be things not mentioned because the author assumed the audience was already familiar with the background of what he was saying. There may be political factors involved in the text as well.

How about where the action was taking place like the country or location?

You may have to find the original meanings of words, including things like jargon and everyday usage. You may also find out that you need to do some more observations, especially if you are examining the original meaning of words. All this plays a role in determining what the author had in mind when he addressed his intended audience and when we get an idea of what that was then we can work on what it means to us today.

Once we get a handle on the interpretation of a passage, then we can move onto the next part of inductive Bible Study. Say this out loud: "What does this mean to me?" – Louder, I can't hear you. "WHAT DOES THIS MEAN TO ME?!"

The point of any Bible study is the application of the passage you are studying. Are there principles you can extract from your work and apply to your life today? God didn't write the Bible just to entertain, bore, fascinate or scare you. He wrote it because He had something to say to you directly. He chose this vehicle to tell you how much He loves you and what He has done just for you.

Some things you will need

It should come as no surprise that there may be a few things you will need in order to successfully complete not only this study guide but any type of Bible study. The first, and don't laugh, is a Bible. A lot of people seem to think they don't really need a Bible in order to study it. They just read a book about the area that interests them. This amounts to a person reading what someone else says about it than learning about it themselves.

Even though this is a workbook, it may be a good idea to have a notebook handy so you can record information that may not be required here. They are also handy if you are making lists, like some words you may explore have a lot of references that you want to keep track of.

Pens, pencils, pencil crayons or highlighters should be an important part of your chest of Bible study tools. A lot of people, myself included, will use color pencils or symbols to mark things in the passages being looked at If they are key words, or present key concepts (If you read the how to study guides you would already know this.). This helps you to remember a Scripture passage the next time you visit it. Having a consistent method of indicating what you discover during your explorations benefits you in that it helps towards retaining what you have learned. By looking at the symbol or the color, you know what the passage is discussing.

Inductive with a twist

Core Elements, is a topical study. Each lesson will concentrate on a particular aspect of our theme. What this means for you is you will be examining many different passages instead of studying one particular book. Each lesson is geared to one specific aspect of our theme. Because you are looking primarily at a topical study, you should expect several exercises per lesson which can include word and verse studies, biographical studies, event and narrative analysis, prophecy analysis, and other goodies designed to challenge you to discover what God has to say about this very important topic.

I am not writing this down just to scare you off, but to let you know and to encourage you to dig deep. This study is not designed to be completed quickly. It is like a several course meal, each lesson to be savored and discussed as you discover the layers of flavors and attempt to identify what is in it. That is the whole point of eating a gourmet feast. It is no different when dining on spiritual food. The Bible has been described as honey. We are encouraged to taste and see that the Lord is good. The Bible is described in the New Testament as milk and strong meat depending on your spiritual maturity level.

The ultimate goal of this particular study for you to get a deeper understanding of what God wants you to do; seek after the things that matter to Him. This guide is also designed in such a way to guide you in finding what the Bible has to say on this topic instead of my commentary on that the Bible has to say. As a result, you will find a lot of questions, charts to complete and, hopefully, not a lot of my own opinion. I don't want to just tell you what the Bible has to say on this fascinating topic. I want you to reach your own conclusions and have your own opinion.

To Exhaust or not to Exhaust

In this type of study there is one important thing to think about. How much information is too much information?

On the surface you may think that I have just contradicted myself somewhere and I probably have in that roundabout way of getting from points A – Z on our journey or wherever we are going.

While it is true the more information we gather on a particular subject, the better prepared we are when it comes time to draw conclusions and applications. However, too much of a good thing, like ice cream or pizza, can lead to heart burn, or in our case, information overload, can lead to getting overwhelmed and discouraged.

So part of the studying process you want to also consider is to be exhaustive or non-exhaustive in your initial observations.

Take for instance our first lesson on exercising faith. When you come to studying this word you will quickly discover it is used about 244 times in the New Testament. Interestingly the Old Testament equivalent is only used 5 times. Does that mean that faith played a lesser role in the Old rather than the New? That is something that you may want to explore.

If you had the inclination and the time, you could look up every single instance where this word is used and determine how it is used, which is an exhaustive approach… and can be quite exhausting, or you can take a sampling of how the word is used to give you a complete picture. Some of your study tools will group them for you like this.

Some words you study may have hundreds or thousands of references. That would take a long time to look up every reference. But you could get a pretty good idea of how the word is used by examining only 15 to 30 references.

If the word you are studying is only used a few, it would be beneficial to look up all those references and see how they were used because you have a smaller sample from which to examine.

There is no arbitrary number on how many or few you should consider when you are doing your study. You want to gather enough information to make you comfortable when you are thinking about your conclusions and applications.

CORE ELEMENTS

Related to the word study would be the topical study. *Ore Elements* is a topical study. Your main tool within the topical study will be the word study. We will be taking a closer look at what God wants us to pursue (word studies). Then as we move to the topical study we may take in a few narratives, events, biographical studies and probably a few more as we get into each lesson.

My Expectations for You

I have included information on topical and word studies for your convenience at the end of this book. They are excerpts from *The Bible School Dropout's Bigger and Better Guide to Bible Study*. They will give you an idea of what to expect as you proceed through your study. They should also give you an idea of how to complete other studies which may crop up in each lesson.

You may have noticed I have made a distinction between lessons and studies. Each lesson comprises of several different studies depending on our topic and the information you should gather and examine to arrive at your destination.

My main goal is not to tell you what the Bible has to say about this subject but to help you determine what it says for yourself. To that end I will ask a lot of questions for you to consider. The specific studies included with each are designed to focus your attention and help you to develop good Bible study methods.

This piece of advice I give often in my other study guides. This is not a race to get to the end. I want you to take your time and enjoy the journey.

Something I've added to this study is a Journal section. As you complete the lessons and set your goals I recommend keeping a personal journal of your progress. The journal is set up so you can record your thoughts, progress, setbacks and successes as you work towards your goals. If you like to keep a journal, you can make the transition to a diary, keeping your notes on your computer, or better yet, blogging your journey online so others can be inspired by you.

Lesson One

Faith

Although the topics we will be examining during the course of this study are in no particular order, exercising our faith is probably the most important core. I think the writers of the New Testament thought so to. They spoke of faith over 240 times. As you complete this and the other lessons I am confident you will reach a similar conclusion.

Faith is fundamental to being a Christian. We are saved by faith. We are to live by faith. God expects us to place our faith in Him. Books have been written about this very important doctrine. Unfortunately we do not have the time to thoroughly explore it in this study.

But by the time we are finished this lesson, you should have a working definition of what faith is, how important it is to our spiritual strength and some ideas for strengthening your faith. Think of exercising faith as the good old core exercise of sit ups; it ain't pretty, it hurts but the end results are worth it. Your posture is straighter, your stomach flatter and you feel great. So let's get to work and feel the burn....

Start by developing a working definition of faith. Complete the *Word Summary* for the word Faith (G4102). Write out your definition here.

What did you learn about faith that you may not have been aware of before?

Complete the *Faith Scavenger Hunt* and answer the questions at the end of the hunt. Feel free to add more verses to the hunt if you come across them.

Summarize your answers for the Scavenger Hunt. Write your answer in a paragraph using first person statements. If you do not have the room, you can use the *Additional Information* page at the end of the lesson.

CORE ELEMENTS

Complete the *Verse Summary* for Hebrews 1:1.

Substance (G5287)

Hope (G1679)

Evidence (G1650)

What do you think the hope the author is basing his argument upon?

What is the hope that is the substance of our faith? Use Scriptures to back your answer. The writer of Hebrews refers to hope five times. Consider these verses in your answer. Use the *Topical Work page* and *Summary* as guides.

What are your conclusions?

Using Hebrews, list the evidence the author provided to support his argument. What are some of the statements he made which would qualify as unseen evidence?

What is the significance of Hebrews 6:11?

What are the two phrases which describe God in this verse?

Why is it important to understand these statements when considering faith is needed to please God?

Complete the summary *By Faith*.

What is the common thread in their demonstration of faith? Look at the original passages where the events occurred to help you answer this question? Provide examples to support your answer.

Abraham is called the Father of faith. Using the *Didactical Summary*, examine Paul's statements about Abraham in Romans 4:1-22.

What did you discover about Abraham's faith?

From what you have studied so far, what is the foundation of our faith?

CORE ELEMENTS

What does God expect of us in the practice of our faith?

The people we looked at pleased God because they believed Him and were obedient to His will. What areas of your life to you feel you have been obedient to God?

What areas do you feel you have not been obedient?

Why?

Do you think your disobedience is a demonstration of a lack of faith?

Support your answer.

What are some practical ways you can exercise your faith?

Prioritize your list. Choose what you consider the most important item on your list.

Using the Takeaway for this lesson, develop a plan to accomplish that goal. Use the SMART Goal objectives. Write a statement beside each step.

Specific:

Measurable:

Attainable:

Relevant:

Time-bound:

Word Summary Date of Study:

Word:	Verse:_____
Strong's Number:	

Definition:

Times Used: ___ Translated as:

Other Sources	Definition(s)

Other Bible References	How Used

Putting it My Own Words

Takeaway

Faith Scavenger Hunt

Passage	What Faith Is	What Faith Does
Genesis 15:1-6		
1 Samuel 12:16		
2 Kings 6:16-17		
Job 19:25		
Psalm 27:1		
Psalm 34:8		
Psalm 57:2		
Psalm 118:5-9		
Psalm145:13		
Psalm 147:10-11		
Proverbs 3:5-6		
Proverbs 22:4		
Isaiah 7:9		
Habbakuk 2:4		
Zechariah 12:5		
Romans 1:17		
Romans 4:3		
Galatians 3:11		
Ephesians 2:8-9		
Ephesians 6:16		

Hebrews 2:9		
Hebrews 10:38		
Hebrews 11:6		
1 Peter 1:5		
1 Peter 1:8-9		
1 John 5:4		

Points to Ponder:

What did you learn about faith that you were not aware of before?

Did this exercise help you develop your concept of faith?

If yes, how did your concept of faith change?

Verse Summary

Date of Study:

Title:	
Verse:	
Strong's Number and Definition(s)	**Used Elsewhere**
Quotation? Yes No	**Summary of Original Passage**
Summary of Verse in Context	
Putting it in My Own Words	
Takeaway	

Topical

Date of Study:

What Does the Bible Say About?		
References	**Details in Context**	**Cross References**
Implied **Direct**		
Implied **Direct**		
Implied **Direct**		

Observations

Overview

In My Own Words

Takeaway

Topical Summary   Date of Study:

Title:	Topic:
Scripture:	Theme:

Key words/phrases:

Verses	Points	Support

Takeaway

By Faith...

Verse	Who	Did What

Didactical Summary

Date of Study:

Passage:		Title	
Author:		Thesis:	
Audience:			
Verse	Argument	Statement	Support
Insight			
Takeaway			

Didactical Summary

Date of Study:

Passage:		Title	
Author:		Thesis:	
Audience:			
Verse	**Argument**	**Statement**	**Support**

Insight

Takeaway

Takeaway

Date of Study:

Passage:	Title:
Key Verse:	Key words:

I think God wants me to know:

How could I apply this to my life:

What steps do I need to do to reach my goal:

My prayer is:

Questions for further study:

Additional Notes:

Lesson Two

Building the Word

There is a lot to be said for not reinventing the wheel and this is one of those times. I first included a bonus study on five ways to build God's Word in our lives in *The Bible School Dropout's Guide to More Bible Study*. I then created a standalone booklet based on the same study called *The Bible School Dropout's Guide to Building the Word of God in My Life*.

So here is the catch. The original study consisted of six different studies; a general overview and then more specific studies on the different ways you can build God's Word. I considered how I could edit the studies to make it smaller without damaging the integrity of the original material and still get the message across.

The study was also designed to be done over a period of weeks rather that in the short time we have to spend on this lesson here. So here is my compromise on this dilemma. I am going to keep the six lesson format, but I am adapting it so the homework is not included. The timetable you set to complete the lesson is up to you.

Study One

Building the Word of God in My Life

Jerry Bridges wrote about the importance of spending time in God's Word in his book, *The Pursuit of Holiness.* He indicated there was not one component to consider, but two. "A disciplined intake of the Word of God not only involves a planned time, it also involves a planned method (pg 102).

He identifies five methods the Bible discusses on building God's Word into our lives; hearing, reading, memorizing, studying and meditating.

Now you may be thinking that may sound like an awful lot of work. In today's society, we have been programmed for instant gratification. This idea has been transferred into the Christian world and we often expect instant spirituality.

However, God does not work like that. He expects us to take the time to get to know Him and grow spiritually according to His will and plan. Just like our physical growth, spiritual growth is an ongoing process.

CORE ELEMENTS

Developing that growth requires self-discipline in order to bring about the desired results. This series of studies will help lay a foundation for the importance of building God's Word and how we can go about doing that.

1. What do the following verses tell us about what God's word can do for us?

Psalms 119:11

Psalms 119:105

Proverbs 24:5-6

Isaiah 33:6

Micah 2:7

Romans 10:17

Ephesians 1:17-21

Ephesians 5:10

2 Timothy 3:1

Hebrews 4:12

2. In the following verses, how do David, Solomon, and Jeremiah Describe God's Word?

Psalms 19:7-11

Psalms 119:103

Proverbs 24:13-14

Jeremiah 15:16

3. What kind of analogy can we draw from these verses?

4. Read the following verses. What are the ways we can build God's word in our lives?

Romans 10:17

Revelation 1:3

2 Timothy 2:15

Psalms 119:11

Joshua 1:8

5. Jesus gives a formula for spiritual growing and building a strong life foundation in Matthew 7:24-28. What is the formula?

(_____ + _____) x _____ = Growth

6. Why do you think people have such a difficult time building God's Word into their lives?

7. What does this statement means to you? "God did not give us His Word to increase our knowledge, but to change our lives."

8. What principle can we apply about building God's Word in our lives from Galatians 6:7?

9. How can we help each other build God's word into our lives?

10. Do you think there is a cost to building God's Word into our lives? What is it?

11. How will building God's Word affect your life?

Additional Notes:

Study Two

Hearing God's Word

I come to the garden alone, While the dew is still on the Roses;

And the voice I hear, falling on my ear,

The Son of God Discloses. C. Austin Miles

We all long to hear God's voice and experience His presence. Yet in our search for this closeness, we often mistake our corporate worship experiences for personal encounters with God. Yet it is the quiet moments, free from distractions, that we truly have the opportunity to experience God.

God demonstrated to Elijah that His presence wasn't in the mighty wind, powerful earthquake, or even in an all-consuming fire. Elijah learned that God is in a still small voice, and he needed to be silent in order to hear it. The psalmist wrote; "Be still and know I am God."

In our daily race, we need to once again be reminded to come away, be silent, and learn to hear the voice of our Master.

Read Deuteronomy 31:10-13

According to the passage, what were the people required to do every seven years?

What was the purpose of reading the Law to everyone?

Read Nehemiah 8:1-12

When in Israel's history did this event occur?

What happened when Ezra opened the book of the Law?

What was the job of the people in verse 8?

What was the response of the people as they began to understand what was being read?

Why do you think they responded the way they did?

What did Nehemiah and the Levites tell the people and why?

What did the people do?

Now read Nehemiah 8:13-18

What did the people discover as they heard the word on the second day?

What did they do?

Read Zechariah 7:8-14

According to this passage, do all who hear God's Word obey?

What was the result of refusal to hear the Word of God?

Read Acts 8:5-8

What was happening in Samaria?

How did the people respond to Philip's message?

Look up the word "heed" (G4337) . What does that word mean?

What was the result of Philip's message?

Read Acts 10:44-48

What were the events just preceding this passage?

What happened to those hearing the Word?

Why would this be happening?

Why were the Jews witnessing the event surprised?

Read Galatians 3:1-6

According to what Paul wrote here, how do we receive the Spirit?

How does the Spirit work powerful works in us?

According to Paul, how was Abraham saved?

What is the passage where this event is recorded?

What is the significance of Romans 10:14?

What was Isaiah's response when he heard God's voice in Isaiah 6:8?

What is God's command in Luke 9:35?

What was the event that occurred when this command was given?

Read John 5:24-29

What does Jesus say in John 5:24?

Who will also hear His voice?

When shall all hear His voice?

What will happen at this point?

Read John 10:1-5

Who do the sheep follow?

Why?

Who don't the sheep hear?

What did the Shepherd do for His sheep?

Read Hebrews 3:7-4:2

What happened because Israel would not hear His voice?

What is the warning here for us?

According to Rev 3:20, what is the promise made to us when we hear and respond to His voice?

Summarize:

According to the passages looked at in this study, list the effects of hearing the Word of God?

According to our study, why is it important to hear God's voice?

Additional Notes:

Study Three

Reading God's Word

"Born to be battered…Underline it, circle things, write in the margins, turn down page corners, the more you use it, the more valuable it becomes."

South Central Telephone Company Yellow Pages Ad.

According to Deuteronomy 17:18-20, what were Israel's kings required to do and why?

Read 2 Chronicles 34:18-21. After the Book of the Law was read to King Josiah, what did he do?

According to Nehemiah 8:2-8, how are we to read and treat the God's Word?

Read Acts 8:27-37. What does God's Word do?

How did Jesus use the Word in the Following passages?

Matthew 12:1-5

Matthew 19:1-9

Matthew 21:41-46

Mark 12: 18-27

Read Luke 4:16-30

What did Jesus do?

How is this event described?

What passage did He read?

Did He read the entire passage?

Why did He stop where He did?

What does this tell us about how Jesus used His Bible?

What was the people's response?

Why do you think they reacted the way they did?

Read Isaiah 34:16-17

What did God command?

What are we reading?

What does God say about what we are reading?

What does say about His Word in Isaiah 55:10-11?

According to the following verses in Psalms 119, what was David's attitude to God's Word?

16

42

113

114

131

161

How does Hebrews 4:12 describe God's Word?

Why do you think this statement is significant?

Thinking about the Scriptures you have considered in this study, what should be your primary focus when reading God's Word?

What kind of attitude should we have when we read the Bible?

As you read God's Word, what should you expect to happen?

Tip of the Day

Howard Hendricks (Living by the Book, video series) gave a list of questions we should ask ourselves when reading Scripture:

1.   Is there an example for me to follow?
2.   Is there a sin I need to avoid?
3.   Is there a promise to claim?
4.   Is there a prayer to repeat?
5.   Is there a command to obey?
6.   Is there a condition to meet?
7.   Is there a verse to memorize?
8.   Is there an error to mark?
9.   Is there a challenge to face?

Additional Notes:

Study Four

Study God's Word

"In Spiritual warfare as in physical warfare, the effectiveness of any weapon is directly proportionate to the efficiency of the one operating it."

A soldier is trained to know every inch of his rifle. He handles it constantly, disassembles, reassembles, cleans and cares for it. When the heat of battle comes, the soldier knows every inch. He knows what can go wrong and how to fix it. His life depends on it.

Our preparation for spiritual warfare should be so thorough. If most people who call themselves Christians had to rely on their Bibles for life and death, they would not survive.

Source unknown

Read Proverbs 2 and answer the following questions.

What are the conditions for understanding the fear of the Lord and finding His Knowledge?

What does the phrase "The fear of the Lord" mean?

What does God give us?

What are the benefits to us for seeking God's knowledge?

CORE ELEMENTS

According to Ezra 7:10 what did Ezra do in order to be used of God?

How do the following passages show us the importance of and the benefits of Bible Study?

Psalms 119:16

Psalms 119:18

Proverbs 25:2

Acts 17:11

Acts 18:24-26

1 Corinthians 2:6-16

1Timothy 4:13-16

1 Peter 1:10-12

Verse Study

2 Timothy 2:15 is a familiar verse when we discuss studying God's Word. Using the Verse Summary chart, do a breakdown of the verse and recreate it in your own words. To make it a bit easier, I have included the Strong's numbers for you.

Verse Summary

Date of Study:

Title: Bible Study	

Verse: Study *4704* to shew *3936* thyself *4572* approved *1384* unto God, *2316* a workman *2040* that needeth not to be ashamed, *422* rightly dividing *3718* the *3588* word *3056* of truth. *225*

Strong's Number and Definition	How is it used elsewhere?
Quotation?	**Summary of the passage**

Summary of Verse in Context

Putting it into my Own Words

Takeaway

Thinking it Through

In your own words summarize what you have discovered in your treasure hunt.

Did you learn something that you were previously unaware of?

What do you think God has impressed upon your heart as a result of this study?

Additional Notes:

Study Five

Memorizing God's Word

"Like Joseph storing up grain during the years of plenty to be used during the years of famine that lay ahead, may we store up the truths of God's Word in our hearts as much as possible, so that we are prepared for whatever suffering we are called upon to endure." – Billy Graham (('Till Armageddon (Minneapolis: Worldwide, 1981), 9), (Morgan, Robert J. :*Nelson's Complete Book of Stories, Illustrations, and Quotes.* Electronic ed. Nashville:Thomas Nelson Publshers, 2000, S. 56

Read Deuteronomy 6:6-9

How does this passage refer to memorizing Scripture?

What else were the Israelites required to do?

What was the purpose of what they were commanded to do?

What point was God making when He instructed the Children of Israel to bind Scripture to their hands and forehead as well as the doorposts of their houses?

How does this apply to memorizing Scripture?

Read the following verses and record the benefits of why memorization is important to our spiritual growth.

Deuteronomy 30:14

CORE ELEMENTS

Psalms 119:11

Psalms 119:105

Psalms 129-130

Proverbs 3:3

Proverbs 7:2-3

Isaiah 48:17-18

Isaiah 51:7

Read John 17:14-17 and Colossians 3:16. What function would memorization of Scripture have in our lives?

Thinking it Through

Summarize what you have discovered during the course of the study.

Has today's study brought out something you may not have been aware of before? What is it?

Is there anything in this study you think God wants you to learn and apply to your life?

Additional Notes:

Study Six

Meditating on God's Word

We often sing the hymn *In the Garden.* In our busy world and lives, we long for a time we can be alone with God. *I come to the garden alone, while the dew is still on the roses.* In the whirlwind we call life we want to hear His voice. *And the voice I hear, falling on my ear, the Son of God discloses.* This song is about meditating on the things of God.

When we first think of meditation, our minds immediately connect it to Eastern mysticism, Buddhism, Yoga and New Age. Rarely, if ever, to we think of this practice when it comes to Christianity and our personal spiritual journeys. Yet the Bible has a lot to say about this misunderstood method of building God's Word into our lives.

The Old Testament alone has 58 references to meditation. The words for meditation are used 25 times in various contexts. The New Testament also has it's say on meditation, both directly in by inference.

Let's take a road trip and discover the blessings meditation can have on our spiritual lives.

There are five words the Bible translates as meditation; four in the Old Testament and one in the New Testament. Fill out the Word Summaries on these words to discover more about this word, what it means and how it is used.

According to the following verses, what is the purpose of meditation?

Joshua 1:8

Psalms 1:1-3

Psalms 4:4

Psalms 16:7

Psalms 19:14

Psalms 35:28

Psalms 37:30

Psalms 62:1

Psalms 77:10-12

Proverbs 15:28

1 Timothy 4:15

Record how the following passages apply the principles of meditation in practical ways. Remember to take context into consideration.

Joshua 1:8-9

Psalms 19:14

Psalms 42:1-2

Psalms 46:10-11

Psalms 77:10-12

Haggai 1:5-7

Malachi 3:16-17

Luke 2:15-19

Luke 2:41-50

Colossians 3:1-2

1 Timothy 4:12-15

Summarize

In your own words, what is meditation?

What are the benefits of meditation?

According to our study, how often are we to meditate?

Did this study open your eyes and mind to something you have never considered before about meditation?

What does God expect you to do as a result of this study?

Word Summary   Date of Study

Word: meditate	Verse: Joshua 1:8	
Strong's Number: 1897		
Definition:		
Times used ___ Translated as:		
Other Sources:	Definitions:	
Other Bible References	How are They Used	
Working Definition:		
Putting it My Own Words:		
Takeaway:		

Word Summary

Date of Study

Word: meditate	Verse: Psalms 119:15
Strong's Number: 7878	

Definition:	
Times used ___ Translated as:	

Other Sources:	Definitions:

Other Bible References	How are They Used

Working Definition:
Putting it My Own Words:
Takeaway:

Word Summary

Date of Study

Word: meditate	Verse: Psalms 5:1	
Strong's Number: 1900		
Definition:		
Times used ___ Translated as:		
Other Sources:	Definitions:	
Other Bible References	How are They Used	
Working Definition:		
Putting it My Own Words:		
Takeaway:		

Word Summary

Date of Study

Word: meditate/ponder	Verse: Proverbs 4:26
Strong's Number: 6424	

Definition:

Times used ___ Translated as:

Other Sources:	Definitions:

Other Bible References	How are They Used

Working Definition:

Putting it My Own Words:

Takeaway:

Word Summary

Date of Study

Word: meditate	Verse: 1 Timothy 4:15
Strong's Number: 3191	

Definition:

Times used ___ Translated as:

Other Sources:	Definitions:

Other Bible References	How are They Used

Working Definition:

Putting it My Own Words:

Takeaway:

Additional Notes:

Lesson Three

Baptism

When we read Matthew 28:16-20, more commonly known as The Great Commission," we learn Jesus has commanded his disciples to preach the gospel and make other disciples and then commands them to baptize these new disciples in the name of the Father, Son and Holy Spirit.

There is a great deal of confusion when it comes to the concept of baptism. Some churches and organizations, baptize infants, others only adults. There are some which practice baptism surrogates where people are baptized for those who have passed on. They are dunked, dipped, sprinkled and water poured over their heads. There are churches which believe water baptism is a necessary step in becoming truly saved.

We do not have time to explore this topic in great detail and there are some very controversial aspects to baptism, based on misunderstanding of the context or making assumptions on unclear passages.

Let's start our study by finding out what this word means. Please complete the Word Study chart for G907.

What is the basic meaning of the word?

Looking at the context of the passages, what are some other ways this word is used?

What are some of the verses which show the normal usage of the word is to immerse, bathe or dip?

CORE ELEMENTS

What are some verses which show baptism symbolically shows purification from sin and spiritual pollution?

What are some verses which show baptism is a public recognition of a belief, or observance? I have provided some suggestions for you.

Repentance – Matthew 3:11

Remission of sins

John's baptism

Death

One body

What are some other reasons a person was baptized in the New Testament?

In Matthew 3:11 John refers to being baptized by the Holy Spirit and by fire. Examine the following passages which provide information to what this is, when it happened (or happens) and the results. Record your results on the Topical Summary.

Matthew 3:11

Mark 1:8

Luke 3:16

John 1:33

Acts 1:5

Acts 11:15-16

1 Corinthians 12:13

Read Romans 6:1-6

What is the symbolic purpose of water baptism?

The book of Acts is unique as it shows the history of the early Church. Part of this uniqueness was it also showed the transition from the Old Testament to the New. There are several passages which indicate this. Look up the following verses and indicate what the difference was.

Acts 1:22

Acts 10:37

Acts 13:24

Acts 18:25

Acts 19:3-4

How did John's baptism differ from the one Jesus commanded the disciples to make?

In looking over your study notes, what conclusions to you have regarding baptism?

Record your findings in the takeaway chart for this lesson.

Word Summary

Date of Study

Word:	Verse:
Strong's Number:	
Definition:	
Times used ___ Translated as:	

Other Sources:	Definitions:

Other Bible References	How are They Used

Working Definition:
Putting it My Own Words:
Takeaway:

Topical

Date of Study:

What Does the Bible Say About?		
References	**Details in Context**	**Cross References**
Implied Direct		
Implied Direct		
Implied Direct		

Observations

Overview

In My Own Words

Takeaway

Topical Summary   Date of Study:

Title:	Topic:
Scripture:	Theme:

Key words/phrases:

Verses	Points	Support

Takeaway

Takeaway

Date of Study:

Passage:	Title:
Key Verse:	Key words:

I think God wants me to know:

How could I apply this to my life:

What steps do I need to do to reach my goal:

My prayer is:

Questions for further study:

Additional Notes:

Lesson Four

Prayer

Prayer is one of those things many Christians assume is a natural. We are talking to God. Right? Yet when you think about it, did anyone teach you what prayer is and there is a right way and a wrong way to pray?

Many Christians have the idea prayer is some sort of never-ending shopping list. God is there to grant our wishes and wants like rubbing some sort of magic lamp. When our prayers aren't being answered, we give up and stop.

From Abraham and Moses to Peter and Paul, the Bible records the personal conversations with God we call prayer. They cover a wide variety of topics and issues.

If you are fortyish or so you probably learned what is called the Lord's Prayer as a child in school. Some denominations have turned it into a liturgical formula which is repeated at rote. What exactly is this prayer? It appears in Matthew 6 and Luke 11. The evidence points to Jesus was teaching people how to pray from attitude to suggestions on what to pray.

I say suggestions because even between these two passages there are some differences which seem to indicate prayer should not be a rote thing we memorize then repeat like some kind of magical formula to invoke a favorable response from God.

So let us examine the Lord's "Model" prayer to find out how to talk to God.

Let's start our study by looking at some of the words we may not be familiar with and with some which we may use regularly without understanding the biblical concept and usage. Complete the *Word* summaries on the following words. As you read through Matthew 6: 9-13 make a note to look up any other words you are unfamiliar with.

Hallowed (G37)

Debts (G3783)

Debtors (G3781)

Indebted (G3784)

CORE ELEMENTS

Amen (G281)

What did you learn about the word *hallow*?

What is the significance of the use of the word *debts* in Matthew and *sins* in Luke?

Is there a difference between forgiving our debtors and forgiving those indebted to us? Explain your answer.

Amen is one of those words which have been transliterated (the word is converted letter for letter) instead of translated. Does knowing the meaning of this word change what you think about it when you are using it? Explain your answer?

When we look at the components of Lord's prayer we need to consider what He meant by each phrase. Complete the *Phrase by Phrase* summary and answer the following questions. There is a column for supporting references. I have listed some for your consideration. Jot down others as you work through this exercise.

What does it say about our relationship with God?

What does this prayer say concerning worship?

What are the things we should be praying about?

What is the key to forgiveness?

Why is this important? (There is a hint somewhere in first John which relates to this question.)

The Bible has much to say in how we are to approach God. Complete the *Check your Attitude* chart.

What does the Bible have to say about our attitude when we approach God?

What do the following attitudes have to do with prayer?

Humility

Persistence

Thankfulness

Worshipfulness

CORE ELEMENTS

Assurance

What are the attitudes which hinder prayer?

Why do these attitudes impact negatively on prayer?

Let's take a look at a couple of prayers in our Bible to see how they compare to the model. Consider Jesus taught two different models of prayer. Also take into consideration the attitude of the person praying. Use the *How do They Stack Up?* chart to help you analyze these prayers.

What did you discover about these three prayers?

What elements of the model prayer did you see in the prayers?

Nehemiah's

Paul's

Jesus'

What did you discover about prayer that you did not know about before?

Thinking about your prayer habits now, what do you think you would do differently?

Complete the Takeaway for this lesson.

Record your thoughts in the personal journal as you complete this study.

Using the Takeaway for this lesson, develop a plan to accomplish that goal. Use the SMART Goal objectives. Write a statement beside each step.

Specific:

Measurable:

Attainable:

Relevant:

Time-bound:

Word Summary

Date of Study

Word:	Verse:
Strong's Number:	
Definition:	
Times used ___ Translated as:	
Other Sources:	**Definitions:**
Other Bible References	**How are They Used**
Working Definition:	
Putting it My Own Words:	
Takeaway:	

Word Summary

Date of Study

Word: meditate/ponder	Verse:
Strong's Number: 6424	
Definition:	
Times used ___ Translated as:	
Other Sources:	Definitions:
Other Bible References	How are They Used
Working Definition:	
Putting it My Own Words:	
Takeaway:	

Word Summary

Date of Study

Word:	Verse:		
Strong's Number:			
Definition:			
Times used ___ Translated as:			
Other Sources:	**Definitions:**		
Other Bible References	**How are They Used**		
Working Definition:			
Putting it My Own Words:			
Takeaway:			

Word Summary

Date of Study

Word:	Verse:
Strong's Number:	

Definition:

Times used ___ Translated as:

Other Sources:	Definitions:
Other Bible References	**How are They Used**

Working Definition:

Putting it My Own Words:

Takeaway:

Word Summary

Date of Study

Word:	Verse:
Strong's Number:	
Definition:	
Times used ___ Translated as:	

Other Sources:	Definitions:

Other Bible References	How are They Used

Working Definition:

Putting it My Own Words:

Takeaway:

Phrase by phrase

Jesus said...	Which means	References
Our Father in Heaven		Luke 11:2 Romans 8:14-17
Hallowed be Your name		Luke 11:2
Your kingdom come		
Your will be done on Earth as it is in Heaven		
Give us this day our daily bread		
And forgive us our debts		1 John 1:8-9
As we forgive our debtors		
And do not lead us into temptation		1 Corinthians 10:13
But deliver us from the evil one		
For Yours is the kingdom		1 Chronicles 29:11
And the power		
And the glory		
Forever		
Amen		

Check Your Attitude, Dudes (and/or Dudettes)!

Reference	Bad Attitude	Vs.	Good Attitude
Matthew 6:5-7			
Luke 11:5-13			
Luke 18:9-14			
James 1:5-7			
James 4:6-10			
Proverbs 3:34			
Matthew 6:14			

How do They Stack Up?

References	Nehemiah	Corresponds yes or no	Model Prayer
Nehemiah 1:1-11			
	Paul		**Model Prayer**
1 Timothy 1:12-17			
	Jesus		**Model Prayer**
John 17:1-26			

Takeaway

Date of Study:

Passage:	Title:
Key Verse:	Key words:

I think God wants me to know:

How could I apply this to my life:

What steps do I need to do to reach my goal:

My prayer is:

Questions for further study:

Additional Notes:

CORE ELEMENTS

Lesson Five

Fasting

In our modern self-centered society, the idea of practicing self-denial is given very little thought. Even among Christians, the concept of fasting as a spiritual exercise is abstract, even non-existent to most and misunderstood by many.

Although you will find more information, examples and reasons for fasting in the Old Testament than the New, it is important not to dismiss it. Fasting is an extension of prayer, a form of worship which is an indication to God of our sincerity and determination to touch His heart.

Like all spiritual disciplines, fasting is open to abuse. Historically it has been associated with the practice of asceticism, the extreme practice of self-denial and abuse based on the assumption such activities makes one more spiritual and acceptable to God. Today, many of those who practice it have the mistaken idea it is akin to a magical-formula designed to force God to grant one's wishes.

So let's take a closer look at this topic; what it means, when it was employed and why consider it as a core exercise in our spiritual fitness regime.

We are going to start where we usually start with these lesson; definitions. Because I'm being a nice guy as I write this lesson I'm including a list of references for you to use as you proceed.

Complete the Word Summaries on the following words.

Fast H6684

Fast H6685

Fasting G3523

Fasting G3521

What did you discover about the practice of fasting?

CORE ELEMENTS

Use the Topical worksheet to record your observations and conclusions about fasting.

What was or were the primary reasons for fasting in the Old Testament? Give some examples and Scripture references.

What attitude or attitudes did fasting imply? Again provide references to support your answer.

What did Jesus have to say about the practice?

How was the practice abused in biblical times?

Why do you think Jesus did not focus on the practice?

What did Jesus have to say about fasting?

Did any of the New Testament writers place a lot of emphasis on fasting?

What is your evidence to support your answer?

What do you think some of the circumstances are which you would feel led to fast?

What did you learn about fasting which you may not have been aware of before?

Using the Topical Summary, create an outline of three to five points about what you learned about fasting. Support your arguments with Scripture.

Complete the *Take Away* Summary.

Don't forget to write at least one entry in your personal journal.

H6684

צום

tsûm

fasted, 12
Judges 20:26, 1Samuel 7:6, 1Samuel 31:13, 2Samuel 1:12, 2Samuel 12:16, 2Samuel 12:22, 1Kings 21:27, 1Chronicles 10:12, Ezra 8:23, Nehemiah 1:4, Isaiah 58:3, Zechariah 7:5

fast, 8
2Samuel 12:21, 2Samuel 12:23, Esther 4:16 (2), Isaiah 58:4 (2), Jeremiah 14:12, Zechariah 7:5

H6685

צום / צם

tsôm

fast, 16
1Kings 21:9, 1Kings 21:12, 2Chronicles 20:3, Ezra 8:21, Isaiah 58:3, Isaiah 58:5-6 (3), Jeremiah 36:9, Joel 2:14-15 (2), Jonah 3:5, Zechariah 8:19 (4)

fasting, 8
Nehemiah 9:1, Esther 4:3, Psalm 35:13, Psalm 69:10, Psalm 109:24, Jeremiah 36:6, Daniel 9:3, Joel 2:12

fastings, 1
Esther 9:31

G3523

νῆστις

nēstis

fasting, 2
Matthew 15:32, Mark 8:3

G3521

νηστεία

nēsteia

fasting, 4
Matthew 17:21, Mark 9:29, Acts 14:23, 1Corinthians 7:5

fastings, 3
Luke 2:37, 2Corinthians 6:5, 2Corinthians 11:27

fast, 1
Acts 27:9

Word Summary

Date of Study

Word:	Verse:
Strong's Number:	
Definition:	
Times used ___ Translated as:	

Other Sources:	Definitions:

Other Bible References	How are They Used

Working Definition:

Putting it My Own Words:

Takeaway:

Word Summary

Date of Study

Word:	Verse:	
Strong's Number:		
Definition:		
Times used ___ Translated as:		
Other Sources:	Definitions:	
Other Bible References	How are They Used	
Working Definition:		
Putting it My Own Words:		
Takeaway:		

Word Summary

Date of Study

Word:	Verse:
Strong's Number:	
Definition:	
Times used ___ Translated as:	

Other Sources:	Definitions:

Other Bible References	How are They Used

Working Definition:

Putting it My Own Words:

Takeaway:

Word Summary

Date of Study

Word:	Verse:		
Strong's Number:			
Definition:			
Times used ___ Translated as:			
Other Sources:	Definitions:		
Other Bible References	How are They Used		
Working Definition:			
Putting it My Own Words:			
Takeaway:			

Topical

Date of Study:

What Does the Bible Say About?		
References	**Details in Context**	**Cross References**
Implied Direct		
Implied Direct		
Implied Direct		
Observations		
Overview		
In My Own Words		
Takeaway		

Topical

Date of Study:

What Does the Bible Say About?		
References	**Details in Context**	**Cross References**
Implied **Direct**		
Implied **Direct**		
Implied **Direct**		
Observations		
Overview		
In My Own Words		
Takeaway		

Topical

Date of Study:

What Does the Bible Say About?		
References	**Details in Context**	**Cross References**
Implied Direct		
Implied Direct		
Implied Direct		

Observations

Overview

In My Own Words

Takeaway

Takeaway

Date of Study:

Passage:	Title:
Key Verse:	Key words:

I think God wants me to know:

How could I apply this to my life:

What steps do I need to do to reach my goal:

My prayer is:

Questions for further study:

Additional Notes:

Additional Notes:

Lesson Six

Giving

A lot of people groan when they see the plate being passed around on Sunday morning. Often referred to as our tithes and or offering, we quickly drop the money or envelop into the dish and send it on. Many times we guiltily pass it on to the next person, not dropping anything into the plate.

People tend to be sensitive when talking about money and giving. Some people give regularly, some give less often, some not at all. Some churches are adamant about passing the plate and tithing, others don't mention it at all. While it's important to support your local church and those who are recognized workers, there are no cut and dried directions on how to do so. Or are there?

The Bible, particularly the Old Testament, has a lot to say about things like giving, offering and sacrifice. Surprisingly it is not always about money. We could spend a lot of time on this topic. From the amount of research I did to prepare this lesson, I could have written a book about it and not just the few pages here. All told the Bible refers to this topic in its various forms over 1,500 times.

I think many of us have assumptions about this area of our spiritual fitness we often miss the main point in giving not only our money, but our time and effort as well. In the New Testament we are not commanded to give or tithe like they were in the Old Testament but the indication was we would be. Even before the Law there was a lot mentioned about people giving and sacrificing. You may argue they are to totally different things, but I think they can be considered two sides of the same coin.

Giving is not just a financial exercise which is a part of good stewardship, but a spiritual exercise as well. There is a lot to say about it and I could continue to write about this topic. But where's the fun in that?

Spoilers...

Wouldn't want to give you too much information and deprive you of the joy of discovering it for yourself.

CORE ELEMENTS

One thing I will state is we don't have the time to study this topic in depth. We won't be able to spend much time looking at the various offerings in the Old Testament, although that would probably make a fascinating study on its own. Um… That's two… I'd better stop there and get on with the study.

First of all let's define some of our words and how we use them. Please note some of these ideas use several different words. These are just a taste. For more in depth understanding, it would be to your benefit to look at the different words which are used.

Complete the *Word* summaries for the following words.

Tithe H4643

Sacrifice H2076

Offer H5927

Offer H6213

Giving G1394

When does the first mention of an offering appear in the Bible?

What are the circumstances behind this first time?

Which offering was acceptable to God?

Why? What Scripture provides this answer?

What does tithe mean?

According to Deuteronomy 14:22-29 what was the purpose of tithing?

Read Malachi 1:7-8, 12-14; 3:8-9. What was happening?

Reading these passages in context – what were God's charges?

Read Matthew 23:23-24 and Luke 11:42-43.

What did Jesus have to say about the Pharisees in regards to their tithing?

How does that relate to what Malachi wrote?

What is the root of the problem?

Read Luke 18:9-14. Complete the *Parable* worksheet. If you are unfamiliar with how to study a parable I have included a how to from my book *The Bible School Dropout's Guide to More Bible Study* at the end of this guide.

According to this parable what is the issue?

What is God's attitude about the Pharisee's attitude? Quote the passage to support your answer.

According to Deuteronomy 28:47 why did the Israelites lose the blessings they were promised?

Are we commanded to tithe in the New Testament?

Why or why not?

Complete the Topical summary for giving. Use the following verses as your starting point:

2 Corinthians 9:17

Philippians 4:15

Romans 12:8

What are some other verses you came across which talk about giving?

What are the principles of giving in the New Testament?

How are they different from the Old Testament? Give examples in your answer.

What principles between Old and New Testament giving are similar? Provide examples in your answer?

In the brief time we have spent studying this topic have you reached any conclusions to the idea giving involves more than just our money? Support your answer with Scripture.

Create a three or four point outline on giving using the *Topical Outline* chart.

Even though we are not commanded to tithe in the New Testament, do you think it is acceptable to practice tithing today? Please make your answer longer than yes or no...

What have you learned about this topic which you may have not known before?

Why do you think this topic would be included in a study of the "core elements?" The answer "I don't know." doesn't

Complete the *Takeaway* for this lesson. Don't forget to record your thoughts and any decisions you have made in your *Personal Journal*.

Word Summary

Date of Study

Word:	Verse:
Strong's Number:	
Definition:	
Times used ___ Translated as:	

Other Sources:	Definitions:

Other Bible References	How are They Used

Working Definition:

Putting it My Own Words:

Takeaway:

Word Summary

Date of Study

Word:	Verse:
Strong's Number:	
Definition:	
Times used ___ Translated as:	

Other Sources:	Definitions:

Other Bible References	How are They Used

Working Definition:

Putting it My Own Words:

Takeaway:

Word Summary

Date of Study

Word:	Verse:
Strong's Number:	
Definition:	
Times used ___ Translated as:	

Other Sources:	Definitions:

Other Bible References	How are They Used

Working Definition:

Putting it My Own Words:

Takeaway:

Word Summary   Date of Study

Word:	Verse:
Strong's Number:	

Definition:

Times used ___ Translated as:

Other Sources:	Definitions:

Other Bible References	How are They Used

Working Definition:

Putting it My Own Words:

Takeaway:

Word Summary

Date of Study

Word:	Verse:		
Strong's Number:			
Definition:			
Times used ___ Translated as:			
Other Sources:	Definitions:		
Other Bible References	How are They Used		
Working Definition:			
Putting it My Own Words:			
Takeaway:			

Parable Summary

Date:

Scripture(s):	Title:

Details:

Context of Parable

Cultural Background:

What is the point?	

Principles:		Support:

Takeaway:

Topical

Date of Study:

What Does the Bible Say About?		
References	**Details in Context**	**Cross References**
Implied **Direct**		
Implied **Direct**		
Implied **Direct**		
Observations		
Overview		
In My Own Words		
Takeaway		

Topical Summary

Date of Study:

Title:		Topic:
Scripture:		Theme:

Key words/phrases:

Verses	Points	Support

Takeaway

Takeaway

Date of Study:

Passage:	Title:
Key Verse:	Key words:

I think God wants me to know:

How could I apply this to my life:

What steps do I need to do to reach my goal:

My prayer is:

Questions for further study:

Additional Notes:

Additional Notes:

Lesson Seven

Serving

Remember this is a Bible study. So we will not be talking about tennis, volleyball, waiting on tables or being a coffee barista. Well if you are doing this study with someone else you may be serving coffee and other goodies...

I must admit when I first started preparing this particular lesson that it would be fairly straightforward. I had picked out a couple of passages to look at and draw some conclusions. But as I got into it, I realized there is more to this topic than meets the eye. Many of our concepts of service and serving are not what the Bible discussed as service.

There are different types of servants. There are paid servants and unpaid servants or slaves. Our culture tends to be negative towards the concept of slavery, yet it was a common practice in both the Old and New Testament eras. The Law dealt with the issues of servants and slaves and the differences between them. Slaves had the right under Jewish law to be treated fairly and with respect. Jewish people who became servants to pay debts were to be set free after 7 years and during the Year of Jubilee. The clock was reset and all servants were free unless they chose to

In the New Testament, The Roman concept of slavery was one of total ownership. The slave was subject to his or her master's will and the master could punish or even kill their slaves for any cause.

Many of the Bible translators chose to use an older term for *slave* because of the negative connotations we have. The term often used in many Bible version is *bondservant*. This can cause a lot of confusion and has led to the concept that as a Christian you have chosen to become a servant for life (more on that later) when in fact the word just means a *slave*.

As you work through this lesson I think you will understand why service should be considered a core exercise to a strong spiritual life.

Take a look at the two main words we will be focusing on in our study. Complete the *Word* summaries for the following words.

CORE ELEMENTS

Servant G1247

Slave G1401

When you have completed the *Word* summaries, complete the *Comparison* chart focusing on these words.

How is G1247 used in the New Testament?

How is G1401 used in the New Testament?

In a sentence or two, what are the differences between these two words?

If You Want to be Great

Read Mark 10:35-45 and complete the *Narrative Summary*.

What does Jesus say about serving?

What is the difference between the serving Jesus does and the serving he told his disciples they would need to do in order to be great in His Kingdom?

It's a Gift

Read Romans 12:1-8. Complete the *Verse* and *Didactical* summaries for this passage. Depending on the version you are using, Romans 12:1 may end the verse with the phrase "…which is your reasonable service (NKJV), "…this is your true and proper worship (NIV), "…which is your reasonable (rational, intelligent) service *and* spiritual worship (AMP) or even "…*which is* your spiritual service of worship (NASB)." Think about if and how considering the phrasing changes the meaning of the verse or enhances it.

What is the definition of the word *reasonable*?

Why do you think presenting ourselves as living sacrifices be our reasonable service to God?

How does that idea change if I am encouraged to present myself a living sacrifice to God my true and proper worship?

How are the two concepts related?

What is the difference between *conform* and *transform*?

What does Paul indicate our attitude should be?

What is the reason for this?

CORE ELEMENTS

What is Paul saying about serving in this passage?

1 Peter 4:10-11 touches on the same theme. What does Peter write about this topic which adds to what you have learned about in examining Paul's words?

Who do You Serve?

Read Roman 6:16-22. Complete the *Didactical Summary*. Remember to keep in mind the context of the passage. You may need to read beyond this passage to understand the context.

Why does Paul consider us slaves to God?

What were we before we became slaves to God?

What are our choices here?

Servant or slave for life

There is a concept in the Old Testament which has carried over to the New Testament and may have created some misconceptions about being a servant. Some of it has to do with the wording used by the translators. Let's explore the concept of the servant for life... or bond servant to see if it plays a part in what we should consider in our service.

 In the Old Testament there were different types of servants. There was the debt-servant, who became a servant to pay off a debt. Usually these servants were set free after seven years and on the Year of Jubilee. Then there was the servant by choice. Then there is the servant who chooses to serve his master for life. Either because of love for his master or his wife and children were also servants and the man did not want to part from them. There were also slaves, who were not Jewish but gentiles, often captured in battle or bought and were considered property.

Complete the *Topical* study on the concept of *What/Who is a Bondservant?* Use the Scriptures in Exodus 21:1-6 and Leviticus 25:39-45. Pay attention to the words which are being used to describe the bondservant. You may want to take advantage of other sources like commentaries to help you in this study.

What is the difference between a servant and a bondservant?

Why would a debt-servant or paid servant choose to become a bondservant?

Which people were considered property?

Why would many Bible translations use the term bondservant instead of slave?

With this information in mind, read Romans 1:1.

How does Paul describe himself?

CORE ELEMENTS

What is the word he uses here?

How Does Paul describe himself in Titus 1:1?

What do we learn about Paul's servant hood in Galatians 1:10

Based on your study here, does Paul consider himself a slave bought and sold in the marketplace or a debt-servant who has chosen to become bonded to his master?

Why have you reached the conclusion you did?

In looking over our study, in what ways are we slaves of God and in what ways are we servants of God?

Whom are we to serve and in what order?

What did you learn about serving which you may have not learned before?

Why would the concept of serving be considered a core exercise to develop a strong spiritual walk with God?

What do you think you would need to do in order to develop more of a servant's heart or frame of mind?

Complete the *Takeaway* for this lesson

Don't forget to record your thoughts about today's lesson in your journal. Why is this important to you and what you are doing to strengthening your core.

Word Summary

Date of Study

Word:	Verse:
Strong's Number:	
Definition:	
Times used ___ Translated as:	

Other Sources:	Definitions:

Other Bible References	How are They Used

Working Definition:

Putting it My Own Words:

Takeaway:

Word Summary

Date of Study

Word:	Verse:
Strong's Number:	
Definition:	
Times used ___ Translated as:	
Other Sources:	**Definitions:**
Other Bible References	**How are They Used**
Working Definition:	
Putting it My Own Words:	
Takeaway:	

Comparison Summary

vs.

Slave	Scripture	Servant

Insight:

Takeway:

Narrative Summary

Date of Study:

Passage:	Title:

Type of narration: Story, Account, Chronology, Information, Backfill

Characters:	Theme:

Details:	Support

Principles:	Illustrates:

Summary:

Takeaway:

Verse Summary   Date of Study:

Title:	
Verse:	

Strong's Number and Definition(s)	Used Elsewhere
Quotation? Yes No	**Summary of Original Passage**

Summary of Verse in Context

Putting it in My Own Words

Takeaway

Verse Summary

Date of Study:

Title:	
Verse:	
Strong's Number and Definition(s)	**Used Elsewhere**
Quotation? Yes No	**Summary of Original Passage**

Summary of Verse in Context

Putting it in My Own Words

Takeaway

Verse Summary

Date of Study:

Title:	
Verse:	

Strong's Number and Definition(s)	Used Elsewhere
Quotation? Yes No	**Summary of Original Passage**

Summary of Verse in Context

Putting it in My Own Words

Takeaway

Verse Summary

Date of Study:

Title:	
Verse:	
Strong's Number and Definition(s)	**Used Elsewhere**
Quotation? Yes No	**Summary of Original Passage**
Summary of Verse in Context	
Putting it in My Own Words	
Takeaway	

Verse Summary

Date of Study:

Title:	
Verse:	

Strong's Number and Definition(s)	Used Elsewhere
Quotation? Yes No	**Summary of Original Passage**

Summary of Verse in Context

Putting it in My Own Words

Takeaway

Verse Summary Date of Study:

Title:	
Verse:	

Strong's Number and Definition(s)	**Used Elsewhere**
Quotation? Yes No	**Summary of Original Passage**

Summary of Verse in Context

Putting it in My Own Words

Takeaway

Verse Summary

Date of Study:

Title:	
Verse:	
Strong's Number and Definition(s)	**Used Elsewhere**
Quotation? Yes No	**Summary of Original Passage**

Summary of Verse in Context

Putting it in My Own Words

Takeaway

Verse Summary

Date of Study:

Title:	
Verse:	

Strong's Number and Definition(s)	Used Elsewhere
Quotation? Yes No	Summary of Original Passage

Summary of Verse in Context

Putting it in My Own Words

Takeaway

Didactical Summary

Date of Study:

Passage:		Title		
Author:		Thesis:		
Audience:				
Verse	**Argument**	**Statement**		**Support**

Insight

Takeaway

Didactical Summary

Date of Study:

Verse	Argument	Statement	Support
Passage:		**Title**	
Author:		**Thesis:**	
Audience:			

Insight

Takeaway

Topical

Date of Study:

What Does the Bible Say About?		
References	**Details in Context**	**Cross References**
Implied Direct		
Implied Direct		
Implied Direct		
Observations		
Overview		
In My Own Words		
Takeaway		

Topical Summary

Date of Study:

Title:	Topic:
Scripture:	Theme:

Key words/phrases:

Verses	Points	Support

Takeaway

Takeaway

Date of Study:

Passage:	Title:
Key Verse:	Key words:

I think God wants me to know:

How could I apply this to my life:

What steps do I need to do to reach my goal:

My prayer is:

Questions for further study:

Additional Notes:

Additional Notes:

Lesson Eight

The Lord's Supper

I think very little thought is given to this simple service. Many evangelical churches have sidelined the Lord's Supper into monthly or less frequent addendum in the rush to get out of the door by noon. Other churches at the other end of the scale have elevated it to an act were the participants receive grace and relief from their current sins.

Somewhere in the middle is the beautiful truth of the Lord's Supper and its importance in our spiritual lives.

This memorial service is known by several names: Breaking Bread, The Lord's Supper, Communion and Eucharist being the most common. It is a recreation of the portion of the last Passover Jesus celebrated with the disciples before his crucifixion. During the meal He stood and blessed the bread, the *Hafikomen*, and passed it on to his disciples. He informed them that this was the representation of his body which would be shortly sacrificed.

He then took the cup of wine which was shared at that point in the service, blessed it and passed it around indicating this was His blood which was blood offering of the New Covenant.

We will be focusing our study mainly on following passages

Matthew 26:26-30

Mark 14:22-26

Luke 22:14-20

Acts 2:42-46

Acts 20:7-12

1 Corinthians 10:15-22

1 Corinthians 11: 20-30

CORE ELEMENTS

Start with the passages in Mathew, Mark, Luke and 1 Corinthians 11. For each of these complete the *Observation and Event* summaries.

What event is associated with these passages?

Who are the people involved?

Where did this take place?

When did it happen?

Looking at these passages again, complete the *Similarities* summary.

What is your explanation for the difference between the four accounts?

Do you think this will affect your conclusions at the end? Why or why not?

Summarize these passages on the *Topical Worksheet* summaries. Include the passages in Acts and 1 Corinthians 10.

When you look over your work so far, what key words or concepts have you discovered?

How does Jesus describe the bread and wine?

According to Jesus what does the bread represent?

What does the wine represent?

What is the New Covenant?

What are the terms of the new Covenant?

Why is the New Covenant more important to us?

The Lord's Supper is not only a ceremony commemorating His crucifixion. As you go over your notes, what are other things it also represents? I've given you a hint to help you...

1.

2.

3.

4.

CORE ELEMENTS

5.

6.

7.

8.

When we look at the new born church in Acts 2, how often did they observe the breaking of bread?

According to the passage in Acts 20 when did the disciples meet to break bread?

What else happened at this meeting?

Take a look at 1 Corinthians 14:26-33. Using this passage and Acts 20 describe how the church met early in its history.

What was the most important element of the early Church meeting?

In comparing it to current church practices, what is the most important element in today's services?

Why do you think the focus has been taken off of the importance the early church placed on this service?

People will present the argument the term breaking of bread meant sharing meal and not to the Lord's Supper. In reviewing the passages you have examined determine if there is enough evidence to determine if the phrase "breaking bread" in these cases only referred to sharing a meal or to the Lord's Supper. Is it possible the term can refer to both?

What did you learn about the Lord's Supper which you may have not been aware of before?

Complete the Takeaway for this lesson.

Remember to create a journal entry on your thoughts about The Lord's Supper.

I enjoyed this study so much, I am going to share my conclusions. They are added on at the end of this lesson.

Observations

Date of Study:

Passage:	Focus:
Asking: Who ☐ What ☐ When ☐ Where ☐ Why ☐ How ☐	
Reference:	**Statement:**

Insight:

Observations

Date of Study:

Passage:	Focus:
Asking: Who ☐ What ☐ When ☐ Where ☐ Why ☐ How ☐	
Reference:	**Statement:**

Insight:

Observations

Date of Study:

Passage:	Focus:

Asking: Who ☐ What ☐ When ☐ Where ☐ Why ☐ How ☐

Reference:	Statement:

Insight:

Observations

Date of Study:

Passage:	Focus:
Asking: Who ☐ What ☐ When ☐ Where ☐ Why ☐ How ☐	
Reference:	**Statement:**

Insight:

Event Summary

Date of Study:

Passage:	Title:	
Time:	Location:	**Support**
Details		
Details from Other Passages		
Details from Other Sources		
Spiritual or Practical Principles		
Take away		

Event Summary

Date of Study:

Passage:	Title:	
Time:	Location:	Support
Details		
Details from Other Passages		
Details from Other Sources		
Spiritual or Practical Principles		
Take away		

Event Summary   Date of Study:

Passage:	Title:	
Time:	Location:	Support
Details		
Details from Other Passages		
Details from Other Sources		
Spiritual or Practical Principles		
Take away		

Event Summary

Date of Study:

Passage:	Title:	
Time:	Location:	Support
Details		
Details from Other Passages		
Details from Other Sources		
Spiritual or Practical Principles		
Take away		

Event Summary

Date of Study:

Passage:	Title:	
Time:	Location:	**Support**
Details		
Details from Other Passages		
Details from Other Sources		
Spiritual or Practical Principles		
Take away		

How are these passages similar?

Matthew 26:26-30	Mark 14:22-26
Luke 22:14-20	**1 Corinthians 11:20-30**

How are these passages different?

Matthew 26:26-30	Mark 14:22-26
Luke 22:14-20	**1 Corinthians 11:20-30**

Topical

Date of Study:

What Does the Bible Say About?		
References	**Details in Context**	**Cross References**
Implied **Direct**		
Implied **Direct**		
Implied **Direct**		
Observations		
Overview		
In My Own Words		

Topical Summary   Date of Study:

Title:	Topic:
Scripture:	Theme:

Key words/phrases:

Verses	Points	Support

Takeaway

Takeaway

Date of Study:

Passage:	Title:
Key Verse:	Key words:

I think God wants me to know:

How could I apply this to my life:

What steps do I need to do to reach my goal:

My prayer is:

Questions for further study:

Topical Outline

Date of Study:

Title: Remember Me	Topic: The Lord's Supper
Main Scripture: Matt. 26:26-30; Mark 14:22-26; Luke 22:14-20, Acts 2:42-46; 20:7; Cor 10:15-22; 11:11-26	Theme: What the Bible teaches about the Lord's Supper.

Key Words and phrases: remembrance, thanksgiving, communion, covenant, will not eat or drink,

Verse	Points	Support
Matt 26:26 Mark 14:22 Luke 22:19 1 Cor 11:24-25	1. A Memorial 1.1 a physical reminder 1.2 His sacrifice 1.3 the shedding of His blood 1.4 the price paid for my salvation	Joshua 4:1-7 1 Peter 1:18-19
Matt 26:28 Mark 14:24 Luke 22:20 1 cor 11:24-25	2. A New Covenant 2.1 covenant sealed with blood 2.1.1 Noah, Abraham, Moses (Law) 2.2 a new one to replace the old one 2.3 a sign of the new covenant 2.3.1 Noah = rainbow, Abraham = circumcision, Moses = Sabbath keeping	Jer 31:31-34 Heb 8-9:22 Gen 9:12 Gen 17:11 Ex 31:13
Matt 26:26-27 Mark 14:22-23 Luke 22:19-20 Acts 2:42-46 1 Cor 11:24-25	3. A Praise 3.1 blessing (eulogeo) = to speak well of, praise, thanksgiving 3.1.1 speaking well of Christ - His sacrifice 3.1.2 speaking well of God - mercy, grace, provision of new covenant 3.2 thanksgiving (eucharisto) = expressing gratitude, 3.2.1 His sacrifice 3.2.2 the New Covenant 3.2.3 salvation 3.3 a celebration	
Acts 2:42-46 Acts 20:7-11 1 Cor 10:16-21		
1 Cor 10: 16-18	4. A Sharing 4.1 communion = fellowship = sharing 4.2 unity of the body 4.3 our unity in Christ 4.4 our disunity with the world 4.4.1 not to partake of the cup/table of demons unbelievers do not partake	1 Cor 12:12-27 1 Cor 14:26 2 Cor 6:14-16

	4.4.2 not to be unequally yoked 4.5 corporate experience 4.5.1 observed every time the disciples gathered together	
1 Cor 11:26	5. A Participation	
	5.1 our privilege as a priest 5.1.1 partake of the sacrifice 5.2 Our offering as priests 5.2.1 praise	Lev 7:6 Matt 26:10
Matt 26:29 Mark 14:25 Luke 22:17 1 Cor 11:26	5.2.2 good works (worship?) 5.2.3 sharing 5.2.4 ourselves 6. A Proclamation	Mark 14:6 Rom 12:1 1 Cor 9:13 1 Cor 14:26-27 Heb 13:15-16 1 Peter 2:9-10
1 Cor 11:17-22 1 Cor 14:26–40	6.1 of His death 6.2 of the gospel 6.3 a witness to the world of the work of Christ 7. An Anticipation	Rom 3:21-26 Rom 5:1 1 Cor 2:1-2 1 Cor 9:14
	7.1 Jesus made a promise 7.2 an act of faith 7.3 looking to the future 8. A Method	Heb 10:22-23 Heb 11:1 Heb 11:6
	8.1 God is a God of order 8.2 self examination 8.3 how not to come together 8.4 how to come together	1 John 1:5-10

Takeaway
When I participate in the Lord's Supper, I am exercising my privilege of being a priest. As a priest I am also offering sacrifices of praise, thanksgiving and worship. I am commemorating the sacrifice of Christ on the Cross and the provisions provided by the New Covenant. By participating, I am showing the unity of the body of believers I am declaring the Gospel and looking forward to the return of My Lord and Saviour.

Additional Notes:

Additional Notes:

Lesson Nine

Sharing Your Faith

If given a choice, I think most Christians would rather have a root canal done without an anesthetic than speak to other people about their faith.

This is one of those topics for which there has been much discussion, books written and internet sources that we are inundated with ways to share our faith without actually talking to people. I remember as a shy teen in high school inconspicuously dropping Chick Tracks in the library, cafeteria, and stairwells; convincing myself that I was witnessing.

I am much older now (not going to tell you how much older...) and I still struggle a lot with sharing my faith with others. Some people are naturals when it comes to witnessing. Others, like myself find it difficult and often remain silent.

There are many different excuses we use from lack of knowledge to fear. However these are fixable. Knowledge is easy to work on. Overcoming the fear takes time and practice. As usual we are not going into a great deal of depth here. At least that is the goal. We don't have the time and space to cover every aspect of sharing your faith. The goal here is to look at what part of the Bible has to say on this subject.

Let's get started and explore the reason why this is a core element in developing a strong spiritual life.

Complete the Word Summary for

Witness G3144

What is the basic meaning of the word?

What is the most surprising thing you learned about this word?

CORE ELEMENTS

List the ways this word is used in the New Testament. Remember to include a Scripture passage to support your answer. Hint: There are at least seven different ways this word is used.

1.

2.

3.

4.

5.

6.

7.

If you found more than seven ways jot them down here; I've left some extra space for you.

Read Acts 1:1-9 and complete the Event and Timeline summaries for this passage. For the timeline, turn the book on its side so the chart is filled out in landscape mode. (Fancy writerspeak for the long edges of the paper are top and bottom.)

What did Jesus tell the disciples what they would be?

When would they become this?

What kind of assistance where they going to be given on order to carry out their command?

Where were they to take their message and in what order?

Read 1 Corinthians 15:1-4.

According to Paul what is this message?

1.

2.

3.

Read 1 Thessalonians 2:4-5.

According to this passage how did Paul maintain the integrity of the Gospel?

1.

2.

3.

4.

What advice does Peter give in 1 Peter 3:15?

What do we need to have in order to be able to give an answer to anyone who asks of us?

Read 1 John 1:1-10. Complete the *Didactical Summary* to discover the line of reasoning he used to build his argument.

Look over your notes on 1 John 1:1-10 and list at least four points of what it means to communicate Jesus to others.

CORE ELEMENTS

1.

2.

3.

4.

Read the following passages and complete the *I Testify Summary* for each of them

John 4:5-42

Acts 8:26-39

Acts 26:1-23

What did you learn about witnessing from these passages?

Jesus:

Philip:

Paul:

You may have noticed there is one more *I Testify Summary.* Spend a few minutes to look over your observations and notes so far in this study. Then think about what you would say if you were talking to someone about your experiences with Jesus. What would your witness be?

In our study what conclusions do you make concerning what our message is?

In what ways is our message communicated to others?

Looking at our study, which passages speak to the following qualities we should strive for in our spiritual walk and communicating our faith to others. Why would these be important points to consider?

Truthfulness:

Clarity:

Consistency:

Honesty:

CORE ELEMENTS

What did you learn in our study on sharing our faith?

Why do you think this was included in our study on the core elements of a strong Christian life?

We only covered a few aspects of sharing our faith. Checking out your personal library, the library, local Christian bookstore or internet, list five sources where you can learn more about witnessing.

1.

2.

3.

4.

5.

Complete the Takeaway for this lesson.

What is one step you can work on which will strengthen this core element in your life?

Don't forget to continue to record your thoughts in your journal. If you have an opportunity share with someone what you have been learning about. Record what you said and the response. Did is go as you expected? Why or why not?

Word Summary

Date of Study

Word:	Verse:		
Strong's Number:			
Definition:			
Times used ___ Translated as:			
Other Sources:	**Definitions:**		
Other Bible References	**How are They Used**		
Working Definition:			
Putting it My Own Words:			
Takeaway:			

Event Summary

Date of Study:

Passage:	Title:	
Time:	Location:	**Support**
Details		
Details from Other Passages		
Details from Other Sources		
Spiritual or Practical Principles		
Take away		

Timeline

Date of Study:

Scripture:	Title:
Event:	Time Frame:

Takeaway

Didactical Summary

Date of Study:

Passage:		Title	
Author:		Thesis:	
Audience:			
Verse	**Argument**	**Statement**	**Support**
Insight			
Takeaway			

I Testify!

Date:

Scripture		Title	
Bearing Witness		Audience	
Location		Purpose	

Context

Verse	Details	Reference

Response of the Audience

Personal Observations

Takeaway

I Testify!   Date:

Scripture		Title	
Bearing Witness		Audience	
Location		Purpose	

Context

Verse	Details	Reference

Response of the Audience

Personal Observations

Takeaway

I Testify!

Date:

Scripture		Title	
Bearing Witness		Audience	
Location		Purpose	

Context

Verse	Details	Reference

Response of the Audience

Personal Observations

Takeaway

I Testify!

Date:

Scripture		Title	
Bearing Witness		Audience	
Location		Purpose	

Context

Verse	Details	Reference

Response of the Audience

Personal Observations

Takeaway

Takeaway

Date of Study:

Passage:	Title:
Key Verse:	Key words:

I think God wants me to know:

How could I apply this to my life:

What steps do I need to do to reach my goal:

My prayer is:

Questions for further study:

Additional Notes:

Lesson Ten

Fellowship

Mention the word *fellowship* and many Christians will automatically think *potluck.*

Food and fellowship go together like peanut butter and bananas. It is an awesome combination: so don't knock it until you have tried it. Especially when is it in a grilled-in-butter peanut butter and banana sandwich dusted with icing sugar. The warm peanutty goodness melting over the bananas... mmm... be right back...

Ok now where was I? Oh, yeah... fellowship.

The idea of gathering for a communal meal is not a bad way to think about what fellowship is. But that is not all of what fellowship is about. There is a larger component which conveys the ideas of community and solidarity; standing together as a group of people with the same interests and goals.

The idea of fellowship is almost exclusively a New Testament concept. Depending on the Bible version, the Old Testament refers to fellowship only two or three times and not in a positive light. While that may be an interesting concept to explore why that is so, it is not the focus of this study.

So, let's consider what fellowship is and why it should be considered a core element in a strong spiritual life.

The first step is to develop a working definition. You are already familiar with this part of our study as we have done it for every lesson. That's right... the *Word Summary*.

Fellowship G2842

Fellowship G3352

What is your working definition of *fellowship*?

CORE ELEMENTS

What did you discover about this word that you found surprising?

What are the other ways this word is used?

Review your notes on 1 John 1:1-10 from the lesson on Sharing your Faith.

What is the basis of our fellowship?

Who is our fellowship with?

What breaks our fellowship?

What restores our fellowship?

Read 2 Corinthians 6:14-18 and complete the *Didactic Summary*.

What kind of fellowship is this?

How does Paul emphasize the type of Fellowship we are to avoid?

What are Paul's reasons for avoiding this fellowship?

Examine your notes and record other things we are to avoid having fellowship with.

Read Romans 15:26, 2 Corinthians 9:13 and Hebrews 13:16.

How is the word translated and used in these passages?

How does this expand our idea of fellowship?

CORE ELEMENTS

Complete the *Topical Worksheet* on fellowship.

Looking over your notes for this lesson create a *Topical* outline for fellowship. Include three or four points with supporting Scriptures. Don't forget to list some points supporting your outline.

What did you learn about your study of fellowship which you may have not realized before?

How has this study changed your ideas of what fellowship is?

Why should fellowship be considered a core element of a strong spiritual life?

Complete the *Takeaway* for this lesson.

Continue to record your thoughts in your *Personal Journal*.

Word Summary

Date of Study

Word:	Verse:
Strong's Number:	
Definition:	
Times used ___ Translated as:	
Other Sources:	**Definitions:**
Other Bible References	**How are They Used**
Working Definition:	
Putting it My Own Words:	
Takeaway:	

Word Summary

Date of Study

Word:	Verse:
Strong's Number:	
Definition:	
Times used ___ Translated as:	
Other Sources:	**Definitions:**
Other Bible References	**How are They Used**
Working Definition:	
Putting it My Own Words:	
Takeaway:	

Didactical Summary

Date of Study:

Passage:		Title		
Author:		Thesis:		
Audience:				
Verse	Argument	Statement		Support

Insight

Takeaway

Topical

Date of Study:

What Does the Bible Say About?		
References	**Details in Context**	**Cross References**
Implied **Direct**		
Implied **Direct**		
Implied **Direct**		
Observations		
Overview		
In My Own Words		

Topical Summary

Date of Study:

Title:	Topic:
Scripture:	Theme:

Key words/phrases:

Verses	Points	Support

Takeaway

Takeaway

Date of Study:

Passage:	Title:
Key Verse:	Key words:

I think God wants me to know:

How could I apply this to my life:

What steps do I need to do to reach my goal:

My prayer is:

Questions for further study:

Additional Notes:

Additional Notes:

Lesson Eleven

Worship

This is one of those topics where we tend to think we know all about it. But do we?

From liturgical forms, such as Roman Catholicism to dancing in the aisles Charismatics, there seems to be as many opinions about what worship is, and how it's done as there are denominations.

The Bible has a lot to say about worship. That's a given. Our job is to define everything it says about worship and boil it down into twenty pages in this lesson... Riiiiiggghttt...

As I was preparing this lesson I had the chance to visit some of my favorite passages. So let's discover why worship is part of our core exercises to developing and maintaining a strong spiritual life.

We are not going to start this lesson with the usual word study. But don't worry, that will come a bit later. The first thing I would like you to do is to write down your own definition of worship. I don't want you to quote Scripture or look it up in a dictionary.

How do you define worship?

To save a bit of time we will concentrate primarily on what the New Testament has to say about worship. I encourage you to take a closer look at the Old Testament concept of worship; unfortunately we do not have the time to explore it here.

The New Testament uses at least five words to describe worship. By examining all five words and how they are used you will get a fairly good definition of how biblical worship is described. Complete the *Word* summaries for the following words.

CORE ELEMENTS

G4352

G4576

G1391

G3000

G2151

When you have completed the *Word* summaries, write a definition which takes into consideration all of the above words.

Read John 4: 19-24. Complete the *Narrative Summary* for this lesson.

What is the question the woman poses to Jesus?

What was the mountain the woman was referring to?

Why did the Samaritans worship at this location?

Why did the Jews turn to Jerusalem to worship?

Do a quick search of Psalms on the word worship. How many times do the writers reference worshiping in or facing Jerusalem?

According to Jesus how will people worship in the future?

Does this form of worship Jesus is describing require a location? Explain your answer.

How does Jesus describe God?

How does this different from the way Jews worshipped God at that time?

Read John 12:1-8. Complete the *Event Summary*. (Parallel passages are Matthew 26:6-13 and Mark 14:3-9)

When did this event take place?

Where did this event take place?

What did Mary do?

Even though the word *worship* is not used in this passage, how do we know this is an act of worship?

Who else at that meal would have had a reason to worship Jesus? Explain why.

CORE ELEMENTS

Read Romans 12:1-2. Complete the Verse summaries.

What does the word *reasonable* mean?

What does the word *service* mean?

What is your take on reasonable service?

Notice that little word *therefore*? It points to the conclusion of an argument Paul has just made. Looking back at Chapter eleven what is or are the arguments Paul made to reach the conclusion he is making?

What is significant about the phrase *living sacrifice*?

What is the difference between *conformed* and *transformed*?

Why is it important to have our minds transformed?

How does this relate to our reasonable service?

Read Romans 12:3-8. How would these verses relate to our reasonable service or our logical act of worship? Comment on each activity.

Based on our study what can we say about worship?

Is worship just about singing on Sunday mornings? Please write more than *yes* or *no*. After all we are entering the interpretation and application stage. It's time to think about the verses we've studied and thought about.

What did you learn about worship which you may have not been aware of before?

In what way(s) was your idea of worship similar to what was explored in this lesson?

In what way(s) was your idea of worship different than what was discussed in the lesson?

Complete the *Takeaway* for this lesson.

Remember to continue to record your thoughts in the personal journal. If your perception of what worship is has changed what might you do to adjust it to what you have learned?

Although I normally do not direct and comment in my study guides (much) I mentioned earlier some of my favorite passages have to do with worshipping God. We briefly looked at Mary in John 12. Jesus was right; of course He was, about the testimony of her actions standing the test of time.

Abraham's act of worship in Genesis 22 where he was obedient to God's request to sacrifice his only son was another passage which stood out for me. Abraham's comment that God will provide an offering for the sacrifice pictured a cross on that same hill where He indeed provided the ultimate offering as a sacrifice on my behalf.

CORE ELEMENTS

Psalm 19 is an amazing declaration of God's very creation crying out in praise of its Creator. What is more amazing when you think about this from a scientific perspective David is writing about light waves. When we see the stars at night and when we feel the warmth of our sun we are bathed in their worship of God.

I used to sing Psalm 95:6-7 and a young person. I bow down and worship God because of who He is and what I am. He is my God and I am his sheep... er... person.

What are some of your favorite worship selections and why?

Word Summary

Date of Study

Word:	Verse:	
Strong's Number:		
Definition:		
Times used ___ Translated as:		
Other Sources:	Definitions:	
Other Bible References	How are They Used	
Working Definition:		
Putting it My Own Words:		
Takeaway:		

Word Summary

Date of Study

Word:	Verse:	
Strong's Number:		
Definition:		
Times used ___ Translated as:		
Other Sources:	Definitions:	
Other Bible References	How are They Used	
Working Definition:		
Putting it My Own Words:		
Takeaway:		

Word Summary

Date of Study

Word:	Verse:	
Strong's Number:		
Definition:		
Times used ___ Translated as:		
Other Sources:	Definitions:	
Other Bible References	How are They Used	
Working Definition:		
Putting it My Own Words:		
Takeaway:		

Word Summary

Date of Study

Word:	Verse:	
Strong's Number:		
Definition:		
Times used ___ Translated as:		
Other Sources:	**Definitions:**	
Other Bible References	**How are They Used**	
Working Definition:		
Putting it My Own Words:		
Takeaway:		

Word Summary

Date of Study

Word:	Verse:
Strong's Number:	

Definition:

Times used ___ Translated as:

Other Sources:	Definitions:

Other Bible References	How are They Used

Working Definition:

Putting it My Own Words:

Takeaway:

Narrative Summary

Date of Study:

Passage:	Title:	
Type of narration: Story, Account, Chronology, Information, Backfill		
Characters:	Theme:	
Details:		Support
Principles:	Illustrates:	
Summary		
Takeaway:		

Event Summary

Date of Study:

Passage:	Title:	
Time:	Location:	Support
Details		
Details from Other Passages		
Details from Other Sources		
Spiritual or Practical Principles		
Take away		

Verse Summary

Date of Study:

Title:	
Verse:	

Strong's Number and Definition(s)	Used Elsewhere
Quotation? Yes No	**Summary of Original Passage**

Summary of Verse in Context

Putting it in My Own Words

Takeaway

Verse Summary Date of Study:

Title:	
Verse:	
Strong's Number and Definition(s)	**Used Elsewhere**
Quotation? Yes No	**Summary of Original Passage**
Summary of Verse in Context	
Putting it in My Own Words	
Takeaway	

Takeaway

Date of Study:

Passage:	Title:
Key Verse:	Key words:

I think God wants me to know:

How could I apply this to my life:

What steps do I need to do to reach my goal:

My prayer is:

Questions for further study:

Additional Notes:

Additional Notes:

Lesson Twelve

Following Jesus

We hear a lot about mentoring. The idea of a more mature person teaching and assisting another person to become successful in a certain area, usually business, has become a common concept in our society. A mentor is simply a wise and trusted counselor and teacher or an influential person.

The concept of mentoring is not something that was new even in Jesus' time. The Old Testament is filled with examples of a mentoring relationship, such as Jethro and Moses, Eli and Samuel, and Elijah and Elisha.

It may surprise you to know the New Testament concept of discipleship is very similar. The teacher would have several pupils or disciples which he would work with to educate them and then send them out to do the same.

Our idea of Sunday school, morning and evening services and midweek prayer meetings was unheard of in the early church. People weren't called to go to church, but to teach people about the gospel, the person of Jesus Christ and how to follow Jesus and how to teach others to do the same.

Jesus had many disciples. There were 120 mentioned in the upper room in Acts 2. Twelve of these disciples he spent more time with and they eventually became the Apostles, the first leaders of the infant Church. The Church grew by over 3000 people on the Day of Pentecost and all in need of learning the Way.

There actually 2 parts to mentoring or discipleship: the student and the teacher. You can't have one without the other and you need to be a learner or student in order to become a teacher. This is also one of those topics which a lot of books have already been written.

There is a common saying today that when the pupils is ready the teacher will present himself/herself.

When we look at the biblical patter it seems the teacher shows himself first and goes looking for the student. Let's explore this core element to a strong spiritual life.

CORE ELEMENTS

There are two primary words we are going to be starting our study with today. They are actually related with one form being the verb and the other a noun. Complete the *Word* summaries on the following words

G3100

G3101

G1321

What did you learn about G3100?

What did you learn about 3101?

How many types of disciples were there in the New Testament? Example: there were disciples of John, Jesus, etc.

Read Matthew 28:18-20. Complete the *Narrative Summary*.

In what order did Jesus instruct his disciples to spread the gospel?

Compare the similar scenes in Mark 16:14-18; Luke 24:36-49; John 20:19-23 and Acts 1:6-8. Record your findings on the *Comparison Summary*. Make note of where and when these events took place.

Did Jesus Give this commandment on more than one occasion?

In comparing the five passages create a *Timeline* showing approximately when Jesus spoke to the disciples for each event.

What did the disciples need in order to carry out their mission?

When did this happen?

Using the second *Timeline Summary*, create an execution timeline. Put the events in the order in which they would happen. For example, He instructed them to wait in Jerusalem for the Holy Spirit. This would be the first step on executing His commands.

Read Hebrews 5:12-14. What is the implication if this passage?

Why do you think teaching others is an important component in following Jesus?

We are going to look at several principles of mentoring and where they are found in Scripture. It will be your job to look up the passages and place them with the correct principle. The answer key will cost you extra... (nah... it's included at the end of the lesson).

Mentoring Principles Scripture Hunt

	Principle				Scripture	People
1	Mentoring requires a trusting, confidential relationship based on mutual respect.		A		Acts 15:36-39	Barnabas, Paul, John Mark
2	Mentors care about those who follow them.		B		2 Timothy 1:3-14	Paul and Timothy
3	Mentoring involves a definite time commitment		C		Acts 9	Barnabas and Paul
4	Mentors should model performances for mentees providing them with opportunities to observe and develop insights.		D		Matthew 10:25	Jesus and the disciples
5	Mentors challenge mentees on their decisions.		E		1 Timothy 1:3	Paul and Timothy
6	A mentoring relationship is planned for enhancing specific growth goals of a mentee		F		Philippians 2:4	Philippians
7	Mentors introduce their mentees to relationships and resources which further development and opportunities		G		Mark 3:13-19	Jesus and The Twelve
8	Mentors follow a servant leadership model.		H		John 1:43-50	Jesus, Phillip, Nathaniel
9	The mentoring relationship ends when the mentee is able to operate independently.		I		John 13:12-17	Jesus and the Twelve

(Ten Principles of Effective Mentoring, n.a.)

(Thomas Nelson, 2001, pp. 109-110)

Now that we have taken a look at the teacher/mentor part of this relationship, it is now time to examine the other half.

By definition a "mentee is the student who needs to absorb the mentor's knowledge and have the ambition and desire to know what to do with this knowledge. As a student, the mentee needs to practice and demonstrate what has been learned." (Canadian Society of Exploration Geophysicists, n.a)

We could spend a lot of time discussing the conditions necessary for the student or mentee. We won't look at every condition, but we will identify a few of them. Working on the chart *Conditions of Discipleship* Look up the references – identify the condition and give a brief sentence on why this condition is important. There is a partial answer key for this one. I provided the condition for the Scripture passage but you are going to have to keep your thinking cap on to provide the reason this would be considered important.

Conditions of Discipleship

Passage	Condition	Reason this is Important
John 1:39		
John 9:22		
Mark 4:11		
John 13:8		
John 15:4		
Matthew 10: 42		
Matt 16:24		
Luke 9 : 23-27		
John 8:31		

What did you discover about this list of conditions that you may not have been aware of before?

Do you think there is a condition for discipleship which was not included in this list? Identify the condition and the Scripture reference to back up your argument.

Complete the *Verse* summaries for the first three references and the *Narrative Summary* for Hebrew 5:11-14. What is their significance?

Timothy 4:12

Philippians 3:17

2 Thessalonians 3:9

Hebrews 5:11-14

Why do you think it is important to transition from student to teacher?

Why is it important to be an example to those around us?

CORE ELEMENTS

What have you discovered about the topic of discipleship which you may have not been aware of before?

Where do you think you are in the process of discipleship? Explain your answer.

Complete the *Takeaway* for this lesson and record your thoughts and decisions in the *Personal Journal.*

Word Summary

Date of Study

Word:	Verse:
Strong's Number:	
Definition:	
Times used ___ Translated as:	
Other Sources:	**Definitions:**
Other Bible References	**How are They Used**
Working Definition:	
Putting it My Own Words:	
Takeaway:	

Word Summary

Date of Study

Word:	Verse:	
Strong's Number:		
Definition:		
Times used ___ Translated as:		
Other Sources:	**Definitions:**	
Other Bible References	**How are They Used**	
Working Definition:		
Putting it My Own Words:		
Takeaway:		

Compare "The Calls"

Matthew 28:18-20	Mark 16:14-18	Luke 24:36-49	John 20:19-23	Acts 1:6-8
Where	Where	Where	Where	Where
Details	Details	Details	Details	Details

Compare "The Calls"

Matthew 28:18-20	Mark 16:14-18	Luke 24:36-49	John 20:19-23	Acts 1:6-8
Where	Where	Where	Where	Where
Details	Details	Details	Details	Details

Timeline

Date of Study:

Scripture:	Title:
Event:	Time Frame:

Takeaway

Timeline

Date of Study:

Scripture:	Title:
Event:	Time Frame:

Takeaway

Verse Summary Date of Study:

Strong's Number and Definition(s)	Used Elsewhere
Title:	
Verse:	

Strong's Number and Definition(s)	Used Elsewhere
Quotation? Yes No	**Summary of Original Passage**

Summary of Verse in Context

Putting it in My Own Words

Takeaway

Verse Summary Date of Study:

Title:	
Verse:	

Strong's Number and Definition(s)	Used Elsewhere
Quotation? Yes No	**Summary of Original Passage**

Summary of Verse in Context

Putting it in My Own Words

Takeaway

Verse Summary Date of Study:

Title:	
Verse:	

Strong's Number and Definition(s)	Used Elsewhere
Quotation? Yes No	**Summary of Original Passage**

Summary of Verse in Context

Putting it in My Own Words

Takeaway

Narrative Summary

Date of Study:

Passage:	Title:

Type of narration: Story, Account, Chronology, Information, Backfill

Characters:	Theme:

Details:	Support

Principles:	Illustrates:

Summary

Takeaway:

Takeaway

Date of Study:

Passage:	Title:
Key Verse:	Key words:

I think God wants me to know:

How could I apply this to my life:

What steps do I need to do to reach my goal:

My prayer is:

Questions for further study:

Additional Notes:

Mentoring Principles Scripture Hunt –Answer Key

	Principle			Scripture	People
1	Mentoring requires a trusting, confidential relationship based on mutual respect.	H		John 1:43-50	Jesus, Phillip, Nathaniel
2	Mentors care about those who follow them.	F		Philippians 2:4	Philippians
3	Mentoring involves a definite time commitment	G		Mark 3:13-19	Jesus and The Twelve
4	Mentors should model performances for mentees providing them with opportunities to observe and develop insights.	D		Matthew 10:25	Jesus and the disciples
5	Mentors challenge their mentees on their decisions.	A		Acts 15:36-39	Barnabas, Paul, John Mark
6	A mentoring relationship is planned for enhancing specific growth goals of a mentee	B		2 Timothy 1:3-14	Paul and timothy
7	Mentors introduce their mentees to relationships and resources which further development and opportunities	C		Acts 9	Barnabas and Paul
8	Mentors follow a servant leadership model.	I		John 13:12-17	Jesus and the Twelve
9	The mentoring relationship ends when the mentee is able to operate independently.	E		1 Timothy 1:3	Paul and Timothy

(Ten Principles of Effective Mentoring, n.a.)

(Thomas Nelson, 2001, pp. 109-110)

Conditions of Discipleship

Passage	Condition	Reason this is Important
John 1:39	Called	
John 9:22	Confession	
Mark 4:11	Given the Secrets of the Kingdom	
John 13:8	Self-Surrender	
John 15:4	Obedience	
Matthew 10: 42	Service/ministry	
Matt 16:24	Follow Christ	
Luke 9 : 23-27	Take up cross daily	
John 8:31	Continue in the Word	

Lesson Fourteen

Holiness

This topic we are going to briefly explore in this lesson is in my estimation one of the most perplexing we face. What is holiness and how do I get it?

The issues of holiness appear very complex and yet so straightforward. God gave us an instruction book: The Bible.

 In the preface to his classic work *The Pursuit of Holiness*, Jerry Bridges said, *"The pursuit of holiness is a joint venture between God and the Christian. No one can attain any degree of holiness without God working in his life, but just as surely no one will attain it without effort on his own part."* (Bridges, 2003, p. 12).

I recommend this book to anyone who is seriously interested in pursuing this topic in more depth.

So let's explore this concept a little bit today and discover why holiness is a core element to a strong spiritual life.

Complete the *Word* summaries for the word or words which are translated holy. Due our brief time on this subject we will be concentrating mainly on The New Testament with a soupçon of Old (That's a fancy word for "a little bit for flavor."). There are over 375 verses using the word holy for 430 times in the Old Testament and 181 times in 169 verses in the New. This doesn't include all of the synonyms and other related words.

After you have defined these words write a brief definition for each of them below. Include the way the word is most commonly used.

G37

G38

CORE ELEMENTS

G39

G40

G41

G2412

G3741

G3742

At its most basic definition the words defined as sanctification or holiness mean what?

Consider the following verses. What do they have to say about sanctification and holiness?

Matthew 5:48

John 17:15-17

Romans 6:22

1Thessalonians 4:3

1 Thessalonians 5:23

Hebrews 12:4

1 Peter 2:2

1 Peter 1: 15-16

To get a better bigger picture of this doctrine it is a good idea to break down into the different components which apply to our lives as Christians. There are generally three stages to sanctification: Positional, Progressive and Perfective.

Positional holiness refers to our position when we become Christians. He are set apart or sanctified when we accept Jesus as our Saviour. Progressive holiness refers to our spiritual walk as believers and perfective holiness is the end result of our faith when we are finally in God's presence.

Using the related passages below as your starting point complete the *Topical* summaries to discover more about the different aspects of holiness.

Positional holiness: 1 Corinthians 1:30; Hebrews 10:10; 1Peter 1:2

Progressive holiness: John 17:19; 1Peter 1:15; Hebrews 12:14;

Perfective holiness: 1 Thessalonians 5:23;

What did you discover about Positional holiness?

CORE ELEMENTS

What did you discover about Progressive holiness?

What did you discover about Perfective holiness?

Of the three areas of holiness which one do we have the most input on? (If you read the next question, you will get the right answer ...)

List at least five references (at least 5...but you can add more) which talk about our part of Progressive holiness. Add a sentence for each reference on why you included it.

Take a quick scan of holiness in the Old Testament. Comment on three verses which show the difference between the expectations of holiness from the Old Testament.

Look for three more verses which demonstrate the similarities of practicing holiness between the Old and New Testaments.

Why do you think holiness should be considered a core element?

During this study what aspect of holiness do feel is your strongest asset?

What do you think you need to work on in this area?

Complete the Takeaway and record your thoughts in your personal journal.

Word Summary

Date of Study

Word:	Verse:
Strong's Number:	
Definition:	
Times used ___ Translated as:	
Other Sources:	**Definitions:**
Other Bible References	**How are They Used**
Working Definition:	
Putting it My Own Words:	
Takeaway:	

Word Summary

Date of Study

Word:	Verse:	
Strong's Number:		
Definition:		
Times used ___ Translated as:		
Other Sources:	Definitions:	
Other Bible References	How are They Used	
Working Definition:		
Putting it My Own Words:		
Takeaway:		

Word Summary

Date of Study

Word:	Verse:		
Strong's Number:			
Definition:			
Times used ___ Translated as:			
Other Sources:	Definitions:		
Other Bible References	How are They Used		
Working Definition:			
Putting it My Own Words:			
Takeaway:			

Word Summary

Date of Study

Word:	Verse:
Strong's Number:	

Definition:

Times used ___ Translated as:

Other Sources:	Definitions:
Other Bible References	**How are They Used**

Working Definition:

Putting it My Own Words:

Takeaway:

Word Summary

Date of Study

Word:	Verse:				
Strong's Number:					
Definition:					
Times used ___ Translated as:					
Other Sources:	**Definitions:**				
Other Bible References	**How are They Used**				
Working Definition:					
Putting it My Own Words:					
Takeaway:					

Word Summary

Date of Study

Word:	**Verse:**
Strong's Number:	
Definition:	
Times used ___ Translated as:	

Other Sources:	**Definitions:**

Other Bible References	**How are They Used**

Working Definition:

Putting it My Own Words:

Takeaway:

Word Summary

Date of Study

Word:	Verse:
Strong's Number:	
Definition:	
Times used ___ Translated as:	

Other Sources:	Definitions:

Other Bible References	How are They Used

Working Definition:

Putting it My Own Words:

Takeaway:

Word Summary

Date of Study

Word:	Verse:
Strong's Number:	
Definition:	
Times used ___ Translated as:	
Other Sources:	**Definitions:**
Other Bible References	**How are They Used**
Working Definition:	
Putting it My Own Words:	
Takeaway:	

Topical Summary   Date of Study:

Title:	Topic:
Scripture:	Theme:

Key words/phrases:

Verses	Points	Support

Takeaway

Topical Summary   Date of Study:

Title:	Topic:
Scripture:	Theme:

Key words/phrases:

Verses	Points	Support

Takeaway

Topical Summary   Date of Study:

Title:	Topic:
Scripture:	Theme:

Key words/phrases:

Verses	Points	Support

Takeaway

Takeaway

Date of Study:

Passage:	Title:
Key Verse:	Key words:

I think God wants me to know:

How could I apply this to my life:

What steps do I need to do to reach my goal:

My prayer is:

Questions for further study:

Additional Notes:

Lesson Fifteen

Love

As we complete our journey together through this study it seems fitting the final lesson on core elements of spiritual growth is on love.

In all fairness, and I mentioned at the beginning of this study, there are many more areas which we could explore under this general topic. But our journey together for now ends here. I hope you enjoyed it as much as I did in writing it.

I think this is subject is near if not at the top of our priorities for developing and maintaining a strong spiritual core. We will be looking as several very familiar passages during the study and I think you will agree with my assessment. We start with faith and love and on those two all else hangs. If we don't have and exercise our faith we have nothing. If we don't have and exercise love everything we do is a waste of time.

So we started our study all those lessons ago with faith; we end our time together with love.

In defining love we naturally turn to 1 Corinthians 13. Some versions use the word *charity*, but it is the same word we define as love. Complete the definition chart *Love Is*.

Based on what you have explored in 1 Corinthians 13, why is it important to exercise love?

Read 1 John 2:3-11 and complete the *Narrative Summary*.

How do we show we know God?

What else do we demonstrate when we are obedient to His commands?

What is the old Commandment John is writing about? List the reference(s).

CORE ELEMENTS

What is the sign of a person who is walking in darkness?

What is the sign of a person who is walking in the light?

Read John 15:12-17. Complete the *Narrative Summary*.

What is the commandment Jesus gave us?

Why did He give this commandment?

What does Jesus call the disciples?

What is the mark of love for a friend?

What is the significance of Jesus' friendship?

What else did Jesus say which is significant?

Why did He choose us?

Read Matthew 22:36-40. Complete the *Narrative Summary*.

According to Jesus, what are the two greatest commandments?

How does He sum up Loving God and loving others?

Based on what you have explored today would you describe love as a concept, a feeling or action? Explain your answer.

What did you learn about love in this study you may have not been aware of before?

Complete the Takeaway for this lesson.

CORE ELEMENTS

Don't forget to continue to record your thoughts about this subject and others in your personal journal. Reflect on what you have discovered during this study and the steps you plan on taking to exercise one or more of these concepts.

Love is...

Verse	Description	Meaning	Support

From my exploration of this passage I learned:

Narrative Summary

Date of Study:

Passage:	Title:

Type of narration: Story, Account, Chronology, Information, Backfill

Characters:	Theme:

Details:	Support

Principles:	Illustrates:

Summary

Takeaway:

Narrative Summary

Date of Study:

Passage:	Title:

Type of narration: Story, Account, Chronology, Information, Backfill

Characters:	Theme:

Details:	Support

Principles:	Illustrates:

Summary

Takeaway:

Narrative Summary

Date of Study:

Passage:	Title:

Type of narration: Story, Account, Chronology, Information, Backfill

Characters:	Theme:

Details:	Support

Principles:	Illustrates:

Summary

Takeaway:

Takeaway

Date of Study:

Passage:	Title:
Key Verse:	Key words:

I think God wants me to know:

How could I apply this to my life:

What steps do I need to do to reach my goal:

My prayer is:

Questions for further study:

Additional Notes:

Personal Journal Entries

The purpose of keeping a personal journal is for you to reflect on what you learned as you worked through each of the studies.

This is different from a normal review in that you are not necessarily answering questions which test your knowledge, ability to recall information or even how well you turn pages back to the lesson in question to find the answer.

I encourage you to give thought to the concepts we discussed and the conclusions you have reached about each topic. Did you feel God was speaking to you in any particular lesson? Did you make any decision regarding how you would work on these areas and the steps you started to make?

This is an extension of the Takeaways. There is no particular order in which to record your thoughts but there is enough space for you to write something for every day of the study assuming you complete one lesson per week.

Personal Journal

| Date: |
| My Goal for this week: |
| |

| Date: |
| My Goal for this week: |
| |

| Date: |
| My Goal for this week: |
| |

| Date: |
| My Goal for this week: |
| |

| Date: |
| My Goal for this week: |
| |

| Date: |
| My Goal for this week: |
| |

Personal Journal

Date:
My Goal for this week:

Date:
My Goal for this week:

Date:
My Goal for this week:

Date:
My Goal for this week:

Date:
My Goal for this week:

Date:
My Goal for this week:

Personal Journal

Date:
My Goal for this week:

Date:
My Goal for this week:

Date:
My Goal for this week:

Date:
My Goal for this week:

Date:
My Goal for this week:

Date:
My Goal for this week:

Personal Journal

Date:
My Goal for this week:

Date:
My Goal for this week:

Date:
My Goal for this week:

Date:
My Goal for this week:

Date:
My Goal for this week:

Date:
My Goal for this week:

Personal Journal

Date:
My Goal for this week:

Date:
My Goal for this week:

Date:
My Goal for this week:

Date:
My Goal for this week:

Date:
My Goal for this week:

Date:
My Goal for this week:

Personal Journal

Date:
My Goal for this week:

Date:
My Goal for this week:

Date:
My Goal for this week:

Date:
My Goal for this week:

Date:
My Goal for this week:

Date:
My Goal for this week:

Personal Journal

Date:
My Goal for this week:

Date:
My Goal for this week:

Date:
My Goal for this week:

Date:
My Goal for this week:

Date:
My Goal for this week:

Date:
My Goal for this week:

Personal Journal

Date:
My Goal for this week:

Date:
My Goal for this week:

Date:
My Goal for this week:

Date:
My Goal for this week:

Date:
My Goal for this week:

Date:
My Goal for this week:

Personal Journal

Date:
My Goal for this week:

Date:
My Goal for this week:

Date:
My Goal for this week:

Date:
My Goal for this week:

Date:
My Goal for this week:

Date:
My Goal for this week:

Personal Journal

Date:
My Goal for this week:

Date:
My Goal for this week:

Date:
My Goal for this week:

Date:
My Goal for this week:

Date:
My Goal for this week:

Date:
My Goal for this week:

Personal Journal

Date:
My Goal for this week:

Date:
My Goal for this week:

Date:
My Goal for this week:

Date:
My Goal for this week:

Date:
My Goal for this week:

Date:
My Goal for this week:

Personal Journal

Date:
My Goal for this week:

Date:
My Goal for this week:

Date:
My Goal for this week:

Date:
My Goal for this week:

Date:
My Goal for this week:

Date:
My Goal for this week:

Personal Journal

Date:
My Goal for this week:

Date:
My Goal for this week:

Date:
My Goal for this week:

Date:
My Goal for this week:

Date:
My Goal for this week:

Date:
My Goal for this week:

Bonus Chapter

Parables: The Stories of Life (Olar, 2010)

There was a Bible College student who once had the opportunity to visit with Ruth Bell Graham. Hoping to glean some words of wisdom from the wife of the world's best known evangelist and preacher, Billy Graham, he asked her for some advice about preaching. Her response was threefold: "Preach expository sermons, keep it short and use lots of illustrations" (Morgan, 2000).

The best remembered sermons are not those which the preacher throws out verse after verse, but those which are filled with illustrations and stories. When a spiritual truth is illustrated by a story, we are more inclined to remember the point the speaker is attempting to make because we can relate the message to something that may have happened to us, or we can see how this truth can be played out in real life. Successful preachers, teacher and public speakers know the value of using stories to help their audience understand their message and to motivate them to action.

Most of the people who wrote the Bible also knew of this important principle: To illustrate spiritual truth in everyday terms. These illustrations are called parables.

Many of us are familiar with parables, as Jesus used this method in much of his teaching. Jesus isn't the only one to use parables. There are many instances where parables are used to convey spiritual truth. Nathan confronted David's sin of adultery by telling it to him in a parable (2 Samuel 12:1-7).

For those of us who grew up going to Sunday school, we were taught that a parable was an "earthly story with a heavenly meaning." Although this is technically correct, there is more to a parable then meets the eye. A little like our last chapter on poetry.

At it basic meaning, the word parable comes from the Greek *parabole* (pronounced like *parabolay*) and means a placing beside or a comparison. It is equivalent to the Hebrew word *mashal*, which means a similitude."

In plain English: A simple story illustrating a moral or a religious lesson. However, it is not necessarily a story, nor is it always simple.

A parable by any other name is a proverb, or an enigma, or a similitude, or whatever...

There are several words in our English Bibles which are all translated from these two words. Often we are not even aware of this when we are reading through a passage. A parable can take on several identities, from pithy one or two-liners to extended allegories.

Depending on the Bible version you are using, proverbs, similies (not smilies!), sayings, maxims, and axioms all mean the same thing: a short statement generally taken as true. Here are a few to consider:

"And one of the same place answered and said, But who is their father? Therefore it became a proverb, 'Is Saul also among the prophets?'" 1 Sam 10:12. KJV

"As the old saying goes, 'from evildoers come evil deeds,' so my hand will not touch you." 1 Sam 24:13 NIV

"One of their own prophets said it best: The Cretans are liars from the womb, barking dogs, lazy bellies. He certainly spoke the truth. Get on them right away. Stop that diseased talk of Jewish make-believe and made-up rules" Titus 1:12-13 MSG

Now, you are probably asking yourself "Didn't we cover proverbs in the last lesson on poetry?"

Well, yes we did. Most of the proverbs we read were written in poetic form and can be can be studied as poetry. In this lesson we are looking at the definition of the words translated as *"parable"* and looking at how it they are used in Scripture. When recognizing types of literature, it is always important to look at the passage in the context of which it is written.

Enigmatic statements are ones that are designed to be puzzling, ambiguous, unexplainable, or simply baffling. They are designed to singe your brain as you work to figure out what the intended meaning is.

"I will open my mouth in a parable;

I will utter dark sayings of old,

Which we have heard and known,

And our fathers have told us." Ps 78:2-3

"Will no all these take up a proverb against him,

And a taunting riddle against him, and say,

'Woe to him who increases

What is not his – how long?

And to him who loads himself with many pledges?' "Hab 2:6

Ezekiel complained to the LORD about the people's responses to his prophecies:

"And I said, 'O GOD, everyone is saying of me', 'He just makes up stories.'"" Ez 20:49.

Allegory

Although not strictly parables, allegories also fall into this category, as they use many of the same elements as a parable. They are often called extended metaphors. You may remember from our lesson on figures of speech that a metaphor is an implied comparison in which a word or phrase primarily used in one sense is applied in another. Paul referred to the lives of Abraham, Sarah, Hagar, Ishmael and Isaac as an allegory in Galatians 4:22-31. Notice Verse 24:

"Which things are an allegory.." KJV

"Which things are symbolic..." NKJV

"These things may be taken figuratively..." NIV

"This illustrates the very thing we are dealing with now." MSG

Paul was using the real-life situation: *"For it is written that Abraham had two sons: the one by a bondwoman, the other by a freewoman through promise."* He draws a spiritual application from the events which actually occurred in history.

People have taken this particular passage to mean that the Scriptures are open completely to an allegorizing or spiritualizing method of interpretation. However, this method opens the door to the Bible being subject to the viewpoint of the interpreter instead of the other way around. Often a person will use a figurative method of interpretation to change the meaning of the passage in question in order to provide Scriptural proof of their argument. Again, the context of the passage should give you an idea of whether or not to take the passage in a figurative or literal sense.

An example of taking the elements of a passage that is to be interpreted in a figurative sense and applying it to a passage that a more normal sense is expected can be found in Joseph's dream in Genesis 37:9. *"Then he dreamed still another dream and told it to his brothers, and said, "Look, I have dreamed another dream. And this time, the sun, the moon, and the eleven stars bowed down to me."*

We know several facts. The first is in real life, the sun, moon and stars do not bow down to each other. The second one, we know that this is the recording of a dream and the imagery should be taken in a figurative sense. Why? Because the normal or literal sense doesn't make any sense!

The interpretation of the dream is provided in the next verse when Joseph's Dad rebuked him. He understood the dream to mean that the family would bow in obeisance to Joseph. When we read the rest of the story, we learn that Joseph became the second in command over Egypt, and his family did bow down to him.

Now take a look at Matthew 24: 29-30:

"Immediately after the tribulation of those days the sun will be darkened, and the moon will not give its light; the stars will fall from heaven, and the powers of the heavens will be shaken. Then the sign of the Son of Man will appear in heaven, and then all the tribes of the earth will mourn, and they will see the Son of Man coming on the clouds of heaven with power and great glory."

When we read this in the context of where we find it and the circumstances surrounding it, we can conclude this passage can and should be interpreted in a normal sense. There is no indication from the context that the sun, moon and stars referred to in this passages represent something other then actual heavenly bodies.

Once again, it is important to pay attention to context. For those of you who are into meditation, repeat after me, "Context. Context. Context."

Dropping the Other Shoe...

There are some distance cousins of parables and allegories that serve much the same purpose, but are based on different elements. The first is the myth. When we talk about myths , and mythology, we automatically think about the stories of the Greek gods, although many cultures have similar stories. These were stories to explain various things such as natural phenomenon, like the sun moving across the sky, human origins, and religious rites. Although there are many people who would like to pass off the Bible as myth and legend, the Bible has no examples of myths.

The other type of literature in this genre is that of the Fable. Most of us are familiar with Aesop's Fables. A fable is a story mean to teach a more lesson. The characters are usually talking animals, but could be other things as well.

The chart below should help show the differences between these genres.

The Stories People Tell					
	Parable	Allegory	Myth	Fable	Riddle
Description	A story of a common event which is used to illustrate a moral or religious lesson	A story in which people, things and events have hidden or symbolic meanings.	A traditional story used to explain natural phenomenon, human origins, religious rites, etc.	A fictitious story meant to teach a moral lesson. The characters are usually talking animals.	A problem or puzzle in the form of a question.
Based on factual events	Yes	Can be	No	No	Can be
Multiple applications	No	Yes	No	No	No
Used in the Bible	Yes	Yes	No	Yes	Yes

Well, how do I study a parable?

When it comes to interpreting parables, I cannot stress just how important it is to put them in the context of the passage they were written. Don't rush to isolate the parables into a forced application of church life or seeking those hidden, spiritual truths. Start with what was going on when the parable is presented.

As a part of the context, pay particular attention to the cultural and customs. Jesus taught by using a lot of parables, but they weren't just illustrations of the lesson. Many of these parables questioned the social norms of the day and He used shock value to grab the attention of His audience. He took the accusations of his enemies and turned the mirror of the truth of God's Word on their souls.

The next thing to keep in mind that, although, parables may have symbolic elements, they commonly only illustrated one main point. So the goal is to seek the truth of the parable instead of speculating on the significance of the details of the parable.

In order to truly appreciate the depth of the truths these parables portrayed, it is also important to leave our western concepts behind when studying them. You will need to have a knowledge of life in first century Palestine. Jesus drew the objects for His lessons from everyday life.

Let's take a look at a parable to see how Jesus accomplished His objectives of presenting the gospel to people when he used parables.

"And behold, a certain lawyer stood up and tested Him, saying, "Teacher, what shall I do to inherit eternal life?"

He said to him, "What is written in the law? What is your reading of it?"

So he answered and said, "'You shall love the Lord your God with all your heart, with all your soul, with all your strength, and with all your mind,' and 'your neighbor as yourself.'"

And He said to him, "You have answered rightly; do this and you will live."

But he, wanting to justify himself, said to Jesus, "And who is my neighbor?"

Then Jesus answered and said: "A certain man went down from Jerusalem to Jericho, and fell among thieves, who stripped him of his clothing, wounded him, and departed, leaving him half dead.

Now by chance a certain priest came down that road. And when he saw him, he passed by on the other side.

Likewise a Levite, when he arrived at the place, came and looked, and passed by on the other side.

But a certain Samaritan, as he journeyed, came where he was. And when he saw him, he had compassion.

So he went to him and bandaged his wounds, pouring on oil and wine; and he set him on his own animal, brought him to an inn, and took care of him.

On the next day, when he departed, he took out two denarii, gave them to the innkeeper, and said to him, 'Take care of him; and whatever more you spend, when I come again, I will repay you.'

So which of these three do you think was neighbor to him who fell among the thieves?" And he said, "He who showed mercy on him." Then Jesus said to him, "Go and do likewise.'" Luke 10:25-37

Most of us who have grown up in Sunday school has heard the story of the Good Samaritan. On your summary you want to give a brief overview of the parable. Now, before you read any further, go and fill out this part of your summary. No Peaking!

- A man (Jewish) was going from Jerusalem to Jericho
- He was attacked by thieves, robbed, beaten, stripped, and left for dead on the side of the road
- A priest (Jewish) was also going to Jericho. He saw the man laying in the Road, crossed to the other side and kept on going
- A Levite (Jewish) also came by, saw the man and also crossed to the other side of the road and kept on going
- A Samaritan came by, saw the man and stopped to help him.
- The Samaritan took ownership of the situation, took the man to a local inn and paid for his stay there while He cooperated.

Now that we have the nuts and bolts of the parable, let's take a closer look at the context of the story. Remember, no looking at the answers until you have done your own work.

- The story follows the return of the 70 disciples He sent out two by two to preach the gospel.
- He commends them for their spiritual insight and thanks the Father for hiding spiritual truth from the so-called wise men of the day.
- A lawyer (Jewish) deliberately poses a question to Jesus, as he already felt he knew the answer.
- Jesus gives the answer in the form of a parable and turns the tables on the questioner.

In order to fully understand the story, we also need to take into effect the history, and cultural significance of the day.

- The lawyer was a theologian. He was familiar with the Levitical law and was arguing from that perspective.

- The question was not a perspective of really wanting to know the answer, but to probe for a weakness in Jesus response.
- Samaritans were despised enemies of the Jewish people. It was unthinkable that a righteous Jew would assist, or even speak to a Samaritan.
- The lawyer's perception of salvation is not faith-based, but works-based. The keeping of the Law is the central tenant.
- Although the Lawyer gives the right answer to the question Jesus asked, he missed the point. Jesus was talking about a relationship with God, and the lawyer wanted a list of rules and regulations.
- The lawyer, wanting to justify himself, asked who his neighbor was.
- Jesus Proceeds to tell the parable.

When we dig a bit further into the parable, we begin to understand that Jesus not only turned the tables on the young theologian, but he also shocked the sensibilities of those who were listening. The fact he made the Samaritan the good guy was a slap in the face of the Jewish people.

His use of the Priest and the Levite was also a dig at the Pharisees, and other people who feel their agendas for God are too important to stop and help someone in need. How often to we find people in need nuisances and interruptions in our busy lives? We see these people, and we hope the best for them, but helping them is someone else's responsibility.

We also learn that our neighbor is not just those people we associate with. Too often we consider our family church family, actual neighbors, or a circle of friends, to be our neighbors. Jesus taught that anyone in need is our neighbor.

Finally, we learn in this parable that truly loving our neighbor involves far more than just saying to someone, "I'll be praying for you, brother." Our love for our neighbors is shown in our compassion, caring and commitment to assist them in any way possible, even if they are our "enemies."

Notice, the lawyer is so taken aback by Jesus' response, he can't even say the word "Samaritan." He can only mumble, "He who showed mercy on him."

How about an Allegory?

When we look at the parable's cousin, the allegory, we need to remember the elements of the story represent something else. Most of the time, the symbolism of the allegory is explained in the context of the passage in which it exists. So there is no need to tiptoe through the flowery fields of speculation.

John 10:1-16 is an excellent example of an allegory. Using your chart, determine was the symbolic elements are.

"Most assuredly, I say to you, he who does not enter the sheepfold by the door, but climbs up some other way, the same is a thief and a robber.

But he who enters by the door is the shepherd of the sheep.

To him the doorkeeper opens, and the sheep hear his voice; and he calls his own sheep by name and leads them out.

And when he brings out his own sheep, he goes before them; and the sheep follow him, for they know his voice.

Yet they will by no means follow a stranger, but will flee from him, for they do not know the voice of strangers."

Jesus used this illustration, but they did not understand the things which He spoke to them.

Then Jesus said to them again, "Most assuredly, I say to you, I am the door of the sheep. All who ever came before Me are thieves and robbers, but the sheep did not hear them.

I am the door. If anyone enters by Me, he will be saved, and will go in and out and find pasture.

The thief does not come except to steal, and to kill, and to destroy. I have come that they may have life, and that they may have it more abundantly.

I am the good shepherd. The good shepherd gives His life for the sheep.

But a hireling, he who is not the shepherd, one who does not own the sheep, sees the wolf coming and leaves the sheep and flees; and the wolf catches the sheep and scatters them. The hireling flees because he is a hireling and does not care about the sheep.

I am the good shepherd; and I know My sheep, and am known by My own.

As the Father knows Me, even so I know the Father; and I lay down My life for the sheep.

And other sheep I have which are not of this fold; them also I must bring, and they will hear My voice; and there will be one flock and one shepherd."

Okay. Let's take a closer look at this passage of Scripture. After we establish the context of this passage, we want to determine what the elements of the story represent. Most of the time, the representations will be obvious. But if it isn't, don't sweat it. Sometimes we aren't given all the answers. So, without peaking, ahhh... you know the drill!

Elements	Represents
Shepherd	Jesus
Sheepfold	The Nation Israel
Doorkeeper	The Prophets/Holy Spirit
Sheep	Israel
Stranger	Pharisees
Thief/robber	Pharisees
Door	Jesus
Hireling/under shepherd	Pharisees
Other sheep not of this fold	The Church

We also need to keep in mind the context of the story. How do we know He is referring to Israel and Pharisees? Well, in chapter 9, we learn He is speaking with the Pharisees. Since the Church is not yet in existence at this time, He would be referring to Israel.

When we look more into the cultural background, we realize the Pharisees claimed to be the religious leaders of the people, yet robbed them of their spiritual heritage. Jesus refers to them as hirelings as they are only in it for the money.

When we look at some of the principles that this story tells, we learn that spiritual insight is only for those who are spiritually discerned.

I am not going to tell you anything else about this allegory. That is part of the fun; to discover God's truth for your self.

And My Final Word (on this Subject...)

Wrapping up this chapter on parables and allegorical literature, it is important to realize there are significant differences. Parables are usually based on real-life events and usually illustrate only one spiritual principle. Allegories use the elements of the story to represent something else. In Scripture, the allegory is usually, but not always, based on historical facts.

As with other types of Scripture it is vital to always work within the context of the passage the parable or allegory is writing in. Pay close attention to the cultural background and the biases of Jesus' audience. Remember, more often than not, Jesus shocked His audience by talking about things that went against the cultural thinking of the day, such as making a despised Samaritan the hero of the story.

Parables and allegories should never be the basis for doctrine or teaching. They were used as illustrations of the principles that were being taught. This is a common mistake and you can run into all sorts of weird and wonderful conclusions if you decide to make this type of literature.

It is also important to make a distinction between allegory and allegorical interpretation. Allegory is a legitimate form of literature that is found in the Bible. Allegorical interpretation seeks to apply secondary meanings to passages of Scripture where it is not warranted. Remember we want to stay within the boundaries of inductive Bible study methods, not wander the fertile forests of our imaginations.

We can learn a lot from studying parables and allegories in their native locations. You may be pleasantly surprised when you take some of these parables, which you learn as a child in Sunday school and look at them using inductive methods.

Parable Summary

Date:

Scripture(s):	Title:

Details:

Context of Parable

Cultural Background:

What is the point?	

Principles:	Support:

Takeaway:

Allegory Summary

Date:

Scripture:		Title:

Details:

Elements	Represents	Support

Context of Passage

Cultural Background

Principles:	Support

Takeaway:

Works Cited

Bridges, J. (2003). *The Pursuit of Holiness.* Colorado Springs: NavPress.

Canadian Society of Exploration Geophysicists. (n.a). Retrieved from
http://cseg.ca/assets/files/students/Mentee-Roles-and-Responsibilities.pdf

Morgan, R. J. (2000). Nelson's Complete Book of Stories, Illustrations, and Quotes. Nashville, TN, USA.

Olar, S. (2010). *The Bible School Dropout's Guide to More Bible Study.* Sault Ste. Marie: Bible School Dropout Publications.

Ten Principles of Effective Mentoring. (n.a.). Retrieved from
http://www.pcrest.com/LO/TI/mentors3.htm

Thomas Nelson. (2001). *What Does the Bible Say About... The Ultimate A to Z Resource.* Nashville: Thomas Nelson Publishers.

www.ingramcontent.com/pod-product-compliance
Lightning Source LLC
Chambersburg PA
CBHW081147090426
42736CB00017B/3221